EXTRAORDINARY
Latinas

VOLUME III
SHATTERING BARRIERS &
DRIVING CHANGE

PRESENTED BY
ILHIANA ROJAS SALDANA &
SANDRA NOEMI TORRES

EXTRAORDINARY LATINAS VOL III
SHATTERING BARRIERS&
DRIVING CHANGE

Published by:
Ilhiana Rojas Saldana
& Sandra Noemi Torres
www.unitedlatinas.com

Editing by Lora Denton
Masters in Clarity | www.mastersinclarity.com

ISBN: 979-8-218-37035-0

Published in the United States of America

No matter how far we stray, life has a way of pulling us back to what truly matters.

To Sandra Noemi Torres, my husband, my two kids, and all my dear friends, thank you for being by my side and supporting me despite the adversities.

I am forever grateful.

Ilhiana

To the Latinas who shatter barriers
To the Latinas who drive change
The world would not move forward without you
It's your voice, your actions your willingness to stand up,
to say something, to do something
to voice your thoughts, to help another
That actually does inspire others to see possibility for themselves.
And that is what makes the world better.
We all heal. We all start shattering barriers.

Thank you.

This life is what we make of it; what we create of it.
When we learn the magic of it.
We learn to play with it.

It's up to you.
It's up to me.

Cambiamos el mundo para lo mejor

TABLE OF CONTENTS

ACKNOWLEDGEMENTS

We express our heartfelt gratitude to everyone who dedicated immense effort to bring this book to fruition, with special recognition for the exceptional co-authors who generously shared their stories and insights, showcasing the Extraordinary Latinas they have become. Your belief in this project and trust in us throughout the journey is truly invaluable.

A heartfelt acknowledgment goes to Lora Denton and Masters in Clarity (www.mastersinclarity.com) for their unwavering support behind the scenes, contributing significantly to the realization of this book.

A profound thank you to our dedicated Board of Directors for their steadfast commitment to the mission of UNITED LATINAS. Your support has played a pivotal role in establishing this platform, ensuring it becomes a lasting avenue to amplify the voices of Extraordinary Latinas in the years to come.

At the core of our beliefs is the idea that we elevate ourselves by lifting others, and we are deeply appreciative of each one of you who has chosen to join us on this meaningful journey.

Ilhiana & Sandra

UNITEDLATINAS
MightyHUB

**Power Up Your Network and
Become a part of the
UL Online Community**

unitedlatinas.mn.co

LEVERAGING OUR STRENGTHS AND OWNING OUR VOICE AND POWER

FOREWORD BY:

ESTHER AGUILERA

As I read the entries of this group of accomplished Latinas, five words came to mind: powerful, resilient, resourceful, and empathetic. In today's changing and fast-based environments, these attributes are needed more than ever in the leadership landscape to navigate what is next for business and society.

The inspiring women in this book -- Yamila, Irene, Liz, Griselda, Sonia, Adriana, Clara Angelina, Dulce, Jennifer Guzman and Jennifer Franco, Maria Gonzalez and Maria Jimenez, Laura Camila, Leonela, Marcy and Paule --

were raw and authentic in embracing and sharing their personal and professional struggles. They poured out their hearts and souls to offer candid portrayals, wisdom, and lived experiences for your benefit. Readers of Extraordinary Latinas Volume III will find the inspiration, strength, and passion to fuel your life and career journey. It is a book you will come back to year after year to help you reflect, find solace, and the strength to persevere.

I also love this cohort's diversity of thought, age, ethnicity, geography, and industry. The authors' stories, drawn from various corners of life, showcase the strength that arises when we acknowledge and appreciate the unique journeys that shape each of us. As leaders, we must always showcase and reflect the rich racial and multi-country representation of what it means to be Latina in the U.S. This anthology not only embraces the common threads that bind us as Latinas but also celebrates our differences and cultural richness - it is these bonds and differences that make us strong. In exploring the multifaceted dimensions of Latina identity, this book serves as a testament to the power of potential of each and every one of us. It challenges stereotypes and underscores the collective strength that arises when Latinas come together.

My personal and professional pursuit has focused on elevating Latinas and Latinos to positions of power. Over my 33-year career as a 2X CEO and 2X Executive Director, I have been at the forefront, leading some of the most consequential organizations for the advancement of Latinos. I have been privileged to work with our Nation's top leaders, from Cabinet Members and Members of Congress to Corporate CEOs and Directors, in each role on a quest to propel Latino advancement. I have shifted lanes in exciting fields from legislative, procurement, and leadership development arenas to corporate governance and wealth creation. With each pivot, I discovered new strengths and learned from my weaknesses. I gained new knowledge, honed my skills as a strategic results- and growth-driven leader, and persevered during the highs and lows of the economy, a pandemic, and social entrepreneurship.

As an undocumented immigrant to this country, the daughter of a landscape laborer and garment worker, and a first-generation college graduate, achieving these feats took a lot of hard work, overcoming low self-esteem, and defying obstacles. I learned to lean into my strengths and embrace new challenges.

In my previous role as CEO of the Latino Corporate Directors Association (LCDA), I was honored to help create the first and largest network of accomplished Latinos at the pinnacle of corporate leadership to become the premier resource for Latino talent primed for the boardroom. I led the rapid expansion of the organization's operations and programs, brand, and influence to increase the presence of Latinos on corporate boards -- including a 10-fold increase in membership and funding. In the process, we created an inspiration and an aspirational movement that challenges the narrative and perceptions about Latinos in the U.S. to one of abundant talent and potential.

There is much to be optimistic about for Latinas in 2024. This book arrives at an opportune time, as several entries on LinkedIn proclaimed 2024 as the year of the Latina. I am encouraged by recent advancements of Latinas named to top posts. Priscilla Almodovar was named CEO[1] and member of the Board of Directors effective at the close of 2022. Fannie Mae is a Fortune 28 listed company, making Priscilla the only currently serving Latina CEO of a F500 company and only the third ever. Adriana Kugler made history[2] as the first Latina/o ever to be appointed as a member of the Board of Governors of the Federal Reserve System, a role she assumed in September 2023. Also, in the last few years, Yvette Ostolaza[3] ascended to the top post at Sidley Austin as Chair of the Management Committee of Sidley Austin, a top 5 law firm in the U.S.

---

(1) https://www.fanniemae.com/about-us/fannie-mae-leadership-team/priscilla-almodovar
(2) https://www.federalreserve.gov/aboutthefed/bios/board/kugler.htm
(3) https://www.sidley.com/en/people/o/ostolaza-yvette

A pioneer in private equity, Monika Mantilla[4] is likely the first Latina founder, managing partner, and CEO of a firm with a 15+ year history of generating company success and value creation. I could go on to name so many pioneering Latinas whose shoulders we stand on today.

Another optimistic trend lies in the business case for Latino inclusion. The economic might of Latinos is stronger than ever. Thanks to studies by the Latino Donor Collaborative[5] (LDC) and reports by McKinsey & Company[6], we can say that Latinos are the indispensable growth engine of the U.S. economy, workforce, and customer base. We are 62.5 million Americans with a purchasing power of $3.4 trillion, and our GDP is equivalent to the fifth largest economy in the world (LDC data)!! Plus, "Latinos accounted for ¾ of growth in the nation's labor force from 2010 to 2020" (LCD data). That only scratches the surface because the Latino potential remains under-tapped. According to McKinsey, Latino consumers are driving growth while their needs go unmet. "Our research estimates that the Latino consumer base has unmet needs of more than $100 billion currently" and if we address the parity gap between Latinos and non-Latino Whites, Latinos have the potential to generate an additional $660 billion (McKinsey report).

Given the spending potential of Latinos, there is an opportunity for Latinas and Latinos to lean in as founders to start and grow businesses that meet these unmet needs. Large corporations that hire and promote Latina and Latino talent are in a better position to understand this consumer's potential and unmet needs. Warren Buffett once said that if you do not have women on your board or in leadership roles, you are playing with half a team, while your competitors outpacing you with a full team.

---

(4) https://www.alturacap.com/
(5) https://www.latinodonorcollaborative.org/original-research/2023-ldc-fast-facts
(6) https://www.mckinsey.com/featured-insights/diversity-and-inclusion/the-economic-state-of-latinos-in-the-us-determined-to-thrive

While we have winds at our back, the playing field for Latinas is not level, as exemplified by three examples. Latinas simply seek the opportunity to compete and achieve results despite drawbacks. For one, Latinas are among the least paid. Here are the facts from the National Committee on Pay Equity[7]: Latinas and Native women are the least paid. For every dollar white men earn, women earn 84 cents, Latinas earn 54 cents, Native Women earn 51 cents, Black women earn 64 cents, and Asian-NHPI earn 80 cents.

Second, in addition to being resilient, Latinas are entrepreneurial but have limited access to capital. Latino-owned companies grew in numbers by 46% since 2007, outpacing the growth among all other demographic groups combined, and between 2007 and 2012, Latina-owned companies grew by 87%, according to the Stanford Latino Entrepreneur Initiative, 2018 article[8]. Yet, based on MSNBC's January 2023 article[9], "There's a venture capital funding gap for Latina Founders." The article cites that women receive less than 2% of V.C. funding overall.

Third, Latinas are the least represented in the top leadership roles. In 2022, Latinas held only 1.2% of seats[10] on Fortune 500 company boards, which is unacceptable when Latinas are approximately 9.2% of the U.S. population. It compares with 22.5% of board seats held by White Women (37.3% of the population), 4.6% for Black women (6.3% of the population), and 1.95 for Asian-PI women (2.8% of the population)—source: Census Bureau 2022 population estimates.

---

(7) https://www.pay-equity.org/
(8) https://www2.deloitte.com/content/dam/Deloitte/us/Documents/us-missing-pieces-7th-edition-report.pdf
(9) https://www.msnbc.com/msnbc/amp/ncna1302279
(10) https://www2.deloitte.com/content/dam/Deloitte/us/Documents/us-missing-pieces-7th-edition-report.pdf

We celebrate the advancement of all women. At the same time, we can't wait for others to solve these inequities. We all must raise our voices to raise awareness and share the facts. It will take each of us working together to lift up and push up Latinas at every level of the workforce pipeline. Make no mistake, there is an abundance of accomplished Latinas, as demonstrated by those profiled in this book.

In a country that offers opportunities and challenges, what we make of it matters. Lean in by leveraging our strengths and owning our voice and power. It is also an opportunity for us to tighten our bonds, reach out our arms to embrace and elevate one another and celebrate the magnificent prism we bring to the world. You see, it is not just a shared language that unites us. It is the understanding that our sisterhood extends across country and continental borders, across cultures, and across time and space itself to bring us together. Hermanas, we are so much stronger together than we could ever hope to be separately.

Why are these books so important? This book series is for the benefit of the current and next generations, to learn from the wisdom and lived experiences shared by these extraordinary Latinas so that future generations may achieve even greater heights. For the women profiled, their purpose for contributing to this book was a passion to pay it forward for other Latinas so that their stories could be a source of inspiration to propel their success. This group of women wants to help build a world where Latinas have self-validating examples and tools to support them on their professional journeys and beyond. Hope is another big theme for them in the book. May their triumph over adversity bring you hope.

Once all women and men in the U.S. take ownership of the gaps and acknowledge the talents of Latinas, we will create a society that values us all. Many of the women offered a "call to action." Here is a compilation of some of mine and their challenges to take action:

- Tell your story and tout your successes.
- Showcase and amplify the success of other Latinas.

- Know the facts. Raise our voices and amplify the numbers to raise awareness about the state of Latinas in the U.S.
- Lift up current and the next generation Latina leaders. Share resources and job opportunities.
- Ask for help and seek resources that lift you up and remind you of your power.

A resounding congratulations to author Ilhiana Rojas and the contributors. As leaders, the commitment to showcasing and celebrating our rich racial and multi-country representation is not just an obligation but a source of empowerment. Through sharing our stories and lifting each other up, we forge connections that transcend borders and create a tapestry reflecting Latina leaders' resilience and brilliance. This book is filled with courageous and inspiring stories of triumph and beating the odds. Let your personal goals and passions guide you, not the misperceptions or views of others. Ultimately, you are the keeper of your destiny by embracing your potential and power. Here are three of my favorite quotes by Sonia Sotomayor:

"Don't let fear stop you. Don't give up because you are paralyzed by insecurity or overwhelmed by the odds; in giving up, you give up hope."

"In every position that I have been in, there have been naysayers who don't believe I'm qualified or who don't believe I can do the work. And I feel a special responsibility to prove them wrong."

"I do know one thing about me: I don't measure myself by others' expectations or let others define my worth."

Thank you, ladies, for your entries and for encouraging us to embrace our potential, fortify a mindset of continuous learning and sharing, and build a supportive community by Latinas, for Latinas.

May you always be able to tap into your innate power at any given moment, no matter the circumstance or obstacle. I hope you feel us celebrating your wins with you and walking by your side through the toughest situations to become a source of strength and inspiration as you chart your path.

Happy reading and all power to you.

~ ~ ~

Esther is a thoughtful, transformational leader known for driving impact and results. A 2X chief executive and 2X Executive Director, she has forged hundreds of strategic partnerships with Fortune 500 companies, institutional investors, search firms, and private equity. As immediate past President & CEO of the Latino Corporate Directors Association (LCDA), Esther built the first, national network of Latino CEOs, corporate directors, and C-level leaders. She oversaw LCDA's rapid expansion to become the premier resource for Latino talent primed for the boardroom to accelerated the conversation of Latino inclusion in America's boardrooms.
Esther has positively impacted DE&I, ESG, and the leadership landscape as a corporate governance leader. Recognized by Diligent as a 2022 Modern Governance 100 Honoree in the category of ESG, Diversity & Climate Trailblazer, she contributes to thought leadership on the intersection of "S&G" of ESG serving on the Advisory Council of NACD's Center for Inclusive Governance, a contributor to #CompetentBoards and #Ceres governance oversight sessions.

~ ~ ~

Connect with Esther:
https://www.linkedin.com/in/esther-aguilera-lcda/

INTRODUCTION BY:

ILHIANA ROJAS SALDANA

Everything starts with a dream. A white canvas of possibilities and excitement. A vision of limitless opportunities, ideas, and adventures. A heart filled with joy.

However, as we start walking the path before us, we encounter challenges, some of the seemingly bright opportunities start closing, and the stepping stones we had envisioned transform from slightly complicated to almost impossible. Still, somehow, we pull ourselves together and persevere, often propelled forward by our commitment to others, our love for our families, or our personal promise to achieve a greater good.

Yet, our stories, remarkable achievements, and extraordinary efforts often go unnoticed. Nevertheless, we continue. As Latinas, many of us find ourselves repeatedly rebuilding from scratch, sighing in silence, and quickly washing away the tears before anyone notices. We can't afford to look back. We can't look weak. Too much is at stake, and we can only hope for the best.

Yet, within this struggle lies immense power. We are resilient, and the opportunities that await us are boundless. We don't have to start from zero every time if we can learn from each other. If we can see our journey reflected in someone else's. If we can see that we are not the only ones and that there is someone else who has experienced similar challenges and has been able to overcome them and reach extraordinary accomplishments, then it will be possible for us to do the same.

When I stepped out of Corporate after a 20-year successful career as an executive in Fortune 500 companies, I didn't know what I was going to do next. I knew I didn't want to continue in Corporate as it was no longer fulfilling, but as the primary breadwinner of my house, would I be able to go on my own and do something different? Maybe it was too late, and I would have to wait for another life to be able to fulfill my dreams.

After many months of sleepless nights filled with tears, fear, and self-doubt, I finally found the courage to take some risks and reach out for help. I started to reconnect with incredible women in my life who I admired throughout my career and also stepped out of my introversion to connect with new people who were doing admirable things and seek their advice.

It was through their stories that I envisioned a new life filled with dreams and possibilities that filled my heart. Although it was very scary to embark on this new journey with two kids about to head into college, yet somehow, I knew I could do it because I wasn't alone. I was surrounded with women who had gone through similar journeys and were accomplished entrepreneurs.

Today, as an established entrepreneur with two businesses and becoming an advisor to many others, I have learned to embrace the fear and challenges and use them as fuel to move me forward rather than hold me back because I know that I am not alone.

This is part of my legacy. To highlight the incredible stories of Extraordinary Latinas and share their inspiring journeys, creating a beautiful tribute to their lives. These women have gone to great lengths to shatter barriers and drive change not only for themselves and those they care for, but also open the path for many women and Latinas to follow.

For decades, our madres, our abuelas, our tias, and many others have overcome barriers and challenges in silence, have broken molds without people noticing, and have opened paths without getting recognition, all so that their families and people they cared for could have a better life.

It's time for us to honor the women who silently laid the groundwork before us and break through to reclaim our power. To stand proud and embrace who we are, and elevate our voice so everyone can hear us.

Sharing our stories is not just an act of empowerment, it is an opportunity to shed light on the hidden aspects of our journeys, fostering a deeper understanding and connection among us. Let's lean on each other's stories, learnings, and accomplishments so we don't start from scratch all over again.

While our professional goals may differ, and we walk different paths, we are united by a common mission – to create a better world for our families and communities. Let's not be afraid to connect with one another, to reach out to those who have paved the way.

Alone, we possess strength and resilience, but together, we are an unstoppable force. Despite the uncertainties that loom in our future, I am more hopeful than ever. I believe in a brighter tomorrow, confident that my children will inherit a better world than the one I was born into – a world shaped by the collective efforts of every remarkable Latina on this shared journey.

I hope that with this book, you will be inspired and empowered by the powerful stories of Latinas who have defied the odds and achieved greatness. Who have dared to challenge the status quo and made extraordinary achievements. I hope each story will provide you with inspiration, learnings, and advice that will encourage you to believe in yourself and to envision yourself as an author contributing to a future edition, embracing your power as an Extraordinary Latina.

In gratitude,

Ilhiana

~ ~ ~

Ilhiana Rojas is a seasoned Business Strategist, Executive and Leadership Transformational Coach, a Diversity & Inclusion Consultant, an Award-winning Advocate for women and Hispanics, a multiple Bestselling Author, and an International Motivational Speaker. She is a possibility thinker and a firm believer that nothing is impossible. Ilhiana uses her 20-plus years of corporate experience and certified coaching expertise to help build resilient, collaborative, and high-performing leaders and cultures. Ilhiana also serves on multiple Boards supporting initiatives that center on empowering women and Hispanic populations.

~ ~ ~

Connect with Ilhiana
https://www.linkedin.com/in/ilhiana-rojas7
www.belivecoach.com
www.unitedlatinas.com
Email: ilhiana@unitedlatinas.com

ADRIANA VACCARO

"Belonging starts when you embrace your own identity and your dreams even if these are different from the expectations that people around you have for you"

\- Adriana Vaccaro

~ ~ ~

Adriana is the CEO and founder of Culture Redesigned, which specializes in creating inclusive and effective cultures where ALL can thrive. She is passionate not only about organizational culture but also about her three sons. She is a bilingual, bicultural, and experienced Human Resources leader specializing in employee engagement, DEI driven organizational culture implementation, change management, and training and development.

~ ~ ~

To Nick, Matteo, and Luca

THE POWER OF A PASSIONATE VOICE

THE JOURNEY

There is nothing more empowering than a burning desire for change!

My formative years were spent at a private all-girls Catholic school in Colombia that went all the way through high school. I was so involved in academics and loved studying so much that I wasn't aware if we were all "the same" in my school in terms of socioeconomic status or if I was simply oblivious to my surroundings.

Then I went to college, and WOW what a wake-up call! I realized that many of my classmates had a level of exposure, wealth, and privilege that wasn't remotely near my sphere. While I grew up in a loving middle-class family with access to private school and vacations, the contrast I discovered in college was quite impactful. I felt like I had entered a whole new world and wasn't sure how I fit in.

I started working full-time the day after my 18th birthday. I had to take two public buses to get to my full-time job by 8 am. I would work until 5 pm and then take two other public buses to get to my college campus. Meanwhile, some of my classmates arrived by airplane! Yes, you read that right. Private clubs, vacation homes, international travel, refined knowledge of art and culture – it all seemed so exotic to me. We seemed to be living in very different realities.

I eventually graduated from college with a double bachelor's degree, a graduate certificate, and, of course, five years of real work experience in organizational development under my belt. And guess what? My fancy friends, with their rich parents and friends in the right places, ended up with much better jobs than I did!!! While I was happy for them, it also felt unfair.

In 2005. I decided to move to Newton, Massachusetts, through a student visa program to learn English. I had imagined that someone with my education and experience would make more money in America than in Colombia. While I did end up making more money, I was shocked to find that my education and experience meant very little in a foreign country. Add to that my accent, which made finding jobs even more challenging. I finally was offered a job at a gas station – yes, that was my first job in the United States!

One day, while working at the gas station counter, a sales manager from the wireless phone company Sprint came to fill up his car, and we chatted. He mentioned he was looking for a bilingual customer service representative, and viola! I was working for him two weeks later.

Within the year, I met a customer who offered me a job as a recruiter for his company. That was the beginning of my career in Human Resources (fun side note: that customer would someday become my father-in-law!). I stayed on the Corporate HR track for 13 years, working at three different organizations until I started Culture Redesigned.

Today, I have so much clarity when I talk about my business; however, when I started, I didn't know how to articulate my value proposition effectively. For all of you getting started on building your own spaces, please know that the lack of clarity is temporary, and as you continue, you will get better and better at sharing your brilliance.

The great thing about organizational culture work is that as society evolves, businesses evolve, and generations flow through the workforce, the cultures we are igniting and sustaining also evolve. Culture is a constant moving target that should be carefully monitored and nurtured.

In retrospect, I can see that my passion was Organizational Culture as far back as 2005 and that everything I did before starting my current practice has made me who I am today. I love being able to genuinely relate and connect with different people from a place of experience and awareness.

Culture Redesigned is dedicated to creating inclusive work environments where ALL can thrive. We focus on creating environments where trust, accountability, and psychological safety are part of daily lingo. We encourage environments where promotions, professional development, and mentorship opportunities are approached from a place of equity, and outputs support equality. While I started as a one-woman show, I now share the privilege of doing this great work with Carina Lawson, a bicultural, trilingual, Executive Productivity Coach, and a group of consultants with different skill sets. Together, we prioritize our clients' results and have ambitious collective goals for growth in the future.

Today, I am so grateful to be doing work that I'm passionate about, and when I look back over my journey so far, I am equally grateful for every step that got me here. I look back at the younger version of me working at the gas station with great pride as she had no idea what adventures life would bring, but she was willing to embrace all of it.

THE LEARNINGS

I had moved to the US alone. In 2007, I had my son Nicholas, and four years later, his father and I parted ways. I became a single mom with a 4-year-old boy and no family around. Looking back, I realize that I wasn't scared, I wasn't depressed, I wasn't lonely, I was just very driven to give my son the best possible life. I didn't want him to have to hustle and struggle the way I had, but I also realize now that hustle is what got me where I am. I do hope he can develop his own grit and passion for excellence even though he has had a lot of privileges that I lacked early on in my life. Funny, I want him to have everything my college classmates had. Full circle.

Now, I want to share some insights about work and a couple of things I want to ensure other Latinas know as early as possible in their careers. Hard work is important, but it's actually not the most essential piece of the puzzle. I have worked so hard my whole life, and if hard work were the only thing that mattered, I would be rich by now.

My first lesson: Yes, do the work and do it to the best of your ability. In my opinion, there is a sense of fulfillment that comes from delivering excellence; however, make sure you receive credit for what you do.

One of the patterns I realized during my corporate career was finding a "white male voice" to share my ideas, projects, and results. I was the only woman and Latina in a couple of companies. When I had a great idea, I would "sell" my idea to that guy that the CEO loved. You know the guy, right? He is usually very good at something, usually sales or operations, is kind and polite and loves credit. I thought my plan was perfect!

My idea would get approved as if it was someone else's idea, which never really bothered me, and then I would get to do the work and see the results that obviously were being presented as "team" or "project" results and not my personal accomplishments. Again, I was initially fine with this model; however, I saw people get elevated, get raises, get promotions, and become influential while I was still generating the next best idea and doing the work.

Once I started my practice as an Organizational Culture Consultant, two things became clear to me:

One, sometimes we hide behind others because we know ideas are better received if they come from them. If we want to be change agents instead of perpetuating stereotypes, we need to become great at presenting our points of view and our ideas to get the credit we deserve. With the credit comes the title, the raise, and most importantly, the ability to lift others as we rise.

Two, people don't buy from the very intelligent consultant. They buy from the person who has delivered significant results. Deliver the results!

Learn to work hard and take the credit for your results with pride.

I also learned that I could find support where I least expected it. Support doesn't always have to be family or lifelong friends. If you allow yourself to lean into who you really want to be, your support system will start to magically appear. I realized that I needed to stop worrying about my life not making sense to others; I had to live it my way. Once I could fully embrace that, I found myself surrounded by like-minded people, eager to support me on my journey!

THE INSPIRATION

Motherhood has been the ultimate inspiration for me. Legacy, changing the future, breaking barriers, those ideas keep me moving. I want my three sons to have an example of fulfillment right at home. I want them to grow up knowing that chasing dreams is fine if you are willing to put in the work and claim your credit. I want them to know that financial stability is important, but family, spirituality, and fulfillment are even more critical.

As a daughter, I wish I could repay my mom for all her sacrifices. She is an example of humility and resilience. She never discouraged my goals and ambitions. In fact, when no one else seemed to be willing to cheer me on, she supported me unconditionally. That support was, at times, and especially after covid, the only energy that kept me going.

I also love reading and could go on and on about it. I think we are the product of our thoughts and our environment, and reading is a way to keep my thoughts going in the right direction. I particularly love Simon Sinek and Steven Covey. You'd be surprised how much you can be inspired by immersing yourself in the work of inspiring and successful people!
If you are anything like me, you may have a long list of goals, aspirations, and priorities. I want a great marriage (thank you to my husband Matt, you are wonderful!), I want to be close to my three sons, I want God and faith in my life, I want to be a really good and supportive daughter, I want to eat healthy, run a thriving business, stay in shape, read at least one book per month, travel, advocate for those who need it, contribute to causes I am passionate about, and enjoy a lot of time by the beach in the summer.

Yes, that is a long list. Over my life, I've realized that I can't make progress in all those areas by relying on only inspiration, but I can rely on discipline and structure. When you create systems that allow you to progress in all the areas that bring you fulfillment, you essentially create an infrastructure that supports you.

THE ADVICE

Believe in your cause.

From a very early age, probably since middle school, I have had a deep sense of pride in my work. I found connection and purpose through my contributions. That feeling was hard to explain when I was in school. Once I joined the corporate world, while I could explain better, it didn't seem to get a lot of traction. The concept of culture, combined with the fulfillment we can get from our work, has been my cause for as long as I can remember.

However, perhaps because I am an immigrant, a woman, a mother, or maybe because I have an accent, I was afraid to pursue that idea. I was hoping for someone to tell me, "Oh what a great idea, Adriana, this is going to be a success!" I was looking for validation or confirmation, but when I mentioned the idea, people would ask, "Why do you want to leave your job?" or "Why don't you just do traditional HR consulting?"

I know culture might not be the first thought that comes to mind when thinking about the longevity of a business, but I firmly believe, and there is enough data and research available to confirm, that culture overrides strategy and process. You can have the best SOPs, outstanding technology, and a great product or service, but your business will suffer without engaged, committed employees. That commitment is achieved through belonging.

I had a similar experience while looking for a sponsor. I thought it was only natural that my first clients would probably be connected to my inner circle, but that wasn't the case. It took a while to find where I fit and where my ideas were met with excitement and support, but by staying dedicated to my cause, I could do just that!

Today, I'm sure you can imagine how proud I am of what I have built. Not only do I have loyal clients who believe in me, but I also have partners, employees, contractors, and a support system of like-minded people. I now have my "business besties," including some powerful Jefas I can call for advice, sushi, or fun. These friends will mention my name and what I do in the rooms I'm not in. I can't help but think how I'd miss out on this amazing support system if I hadn't embarked on this journey. This is a long way to tell you, Querida, that if I can do it with all my baggage, relying on my passion, discipline, and constant learning, anyone can do it – including you!

Today, I love sharing my cause! Culture is how we do things when nobody is watching; culture drives engagement, which is that emotional connection we create with our work. Creating cultures where ALL can thrive is my passion; I only wish I had chased that dream sooner. Believing in your cause will motivate you to chase your dreams, even in the face of discouragement and obstacles.

Keep striving for excellence while leaning into discomfort.

There are many things I have done with discomfort. The great lesson in discomfort is the reliability of practice. It never goes unnoticed. The more you do the thing, the better you get at it. I remember the first time I presented to a large audience, the first time I sent a proposal, and the first time I was pitching my services. Was it perfect? Not at all. Was it worth it? Absolutely.

When you keep doing "the thing," eventually "the thing" becomes your expertise. If you have a cause, believe in something, and want to get good at something, just keep practicing. Put the time and the work in, even if nobody is watching.

Nothing is more fulfilling than realizing your own growth by serving others to the best of your ability. When I am working with clients, I am doing what

I love. It fills my soul, is enjoyable, and is now easy for me. I have developed confidence in my craft by doing it with discomfort.

Work on your craft! Don't wait for an opportunity, a break, or a handout.

Whatever it is you want to do, lean into it, embrace imperfection, keep practicing, learning, making mistakes, and growing. I have learned that we spend way too much time wishing we were ready. We all have a unique ability, and the best way to find "it" is by taking consistent action.

I know what you might think: What if I don't know what I want to do? As you keep taking action, you will get closer to your zone of genius. And in the worst-case scenario, you will be clear on what you don't want to do. It is like kissing a couple of frogs before the prince(ss). The wonderful thing about action is the fact that it keeps you in a state of evolution and growth.

THE PATH FORWARD

It's important to me to share my story and the importance of embracing our own identity. When we are a little different, think a little different, or sound different, we can get caught up in the false idea that we need to want what others want for us. We tend to borrow the dreams and aspirations of those around us to match some sort of standard.

Achieving someone else's dream will bring zero fulfillment to your life! I wish I had known that when I was younger. I was always working towards satisfying someone else's opinion of me because I wanted to fit in. I wanted to experience belonging, I wanted to be part of something. What I know now is that belonging starts when you embrace your identity and dreams, even if they are different from the expectations of people around you.

ABOUT ADRIANA

Adriana is the CEO and Founder of Culture Redesigned. She specializes in helping companies amplify diversity, equity, and inclusion through organizational culture. Rather than traditional consulting and training techniques, her company uses Behavioral Science Data to align Human Capital with Business Results. Adriana is a bilingual, bicultural, and experienced Human Resources leader. Her areas of expertise include employee engagement, DEI strategy, change management, and training and development.

Born in Colombia and a naturalized citizen of the United States, Adriana earned a Bachelor of Science in Marketing and Advertising and a Master of Business Administration. Adriana is a Senior Certified Professional by the Society of HR Management, Certified Executive Coach, Six Sigma Black Belt, Certified PI Partner, and a Delta Mu Delta Honor Society of International Business member.

Learn more and connect with Adriana at:

https://www.linkedin.com/in/adrianavaccaro/

https://cultureredesigned.com/

Download our guide "Redefining Organizational Culture for the Modern Workplace":

http://bit.ly/redefine-culture

CLARA ANGELINA DIAZ-ANDERSON

"You can be a co-creator of your life through a deep understanding and merging of who you are, who you want to be and who you are called to become."

\- Clara Angelina Diaz-Anderson

~ ~ ~

A certified Master Coach for over 15 years, Clara is the founder of
ClaraFying Coaching and Consulting Institute where her team of executive
and career coaches, consultants, and facilitators, lead personal,
professional, business, and culture transformation projects for a premier
clientele globally. She teaches; Authentic Leadership and Executive
Coaching Mastery at Harvard University School of Professional
Development and Executive Education.

Clara is originally from the Dominican Republic, and her mission is to help
people awaken to their innate power and use that knowledge for the good
of all.. She is a published author of the book "Create Your Best Year One
Day At A Time ".

~ ~ ~

This chapter is dedicated to my daughter Angelina, my deepest inspiration
to honor my roots, live with authenticity and create a positive legacy.

FROM CONTEMPLATION TO ACTION: FINDING YOUR AUTHENTIC SELF

THE JOURNEY

I am Dominican. I was born and grew up in the Dominican Republic until the age of eight, where I went by the name Angelina. My Dominican nickname was "antenita de vinil," from the show El Chabo del 8, a vinyl antenna to be exact, because I was always so aware of my surroundings and what people around me were saying and doing. I think I was born with more of a heightened awareness than the average child. This severe case of hyper-vigilance would later become one of my superpowers: Claircognizance. This term describes a spiritual 6th sense defined by having a deep and almost instant knowledge about people, things, and situations. It goes beyond the apparent and available information to others. It's a profound intuition, usually accompanied by a physical gut sensation that what you perceive is true.

In my case it turns out that there can be spiritual benefits to a chaotic childhood, being born on a beautifully lush island, colonized by patriarchy, nurtured and fed by women who have traditional oppressive roles, and still manage to do everything with grace, beauty, and gratitude to God, first and foremost just the way they have been taught for generations. I now know that the pain of trauma can transform into heightened abilities that I have chosen to use for good.

Today, this heightened awareness is one of my superpowers as a social entrepreneur, executive leadership coach, and educator at Harvard University School of Professional Development and Executive Education. It has also supported me in creating my company, Clarafying Coaching and Consulting Institute, and as a published author of two books, Create Your Best Year (available in both English and Spanish) and my forthcoming book, will support heart-centered leaders to use their powers consciously, as systemic change makers and global citizens.

As a child, I constantly asked why everything felt so unfair. This level of inquiry brewed my determination to fix the blatant injustices I saw. I was naturally curious and highly observant of how people treated each other. For example, I noticed when the men in the house got the more significant piece of meat, leaving the children and women with the bonier portions. I also noticed that the women did more housework while the boys got to play more.

At the age of six, I remember making a promise to myself to live a different life from the unhealed family I was surrounded by. I was determined not to be a byproduct of my surroundings. At the time, I didn't know that all I was experiencing and witnessing would lead me to where I am today.

By paying attention to the things I didn't want, I could make conscious choices later on to avoid those things and instead embrace a new way forward, different from the environment I'd grown up in. I knew that I would not accept domestic violence at home, gender inequality, and blatant acceptance of ignorance and tradition. As a young girl, I observed the women in my life dealing with cheating partners, being solely responsible for the housework and child-rearing, all while being miserable and complaining constantly. I saw hopelessness in competent women who felt bound by these dynamics. I remember every single Saturday morning, instead of enjoying extracurricular activities, my siblings and would be forced by my father to stay home and deep clean the house simply because it was a custom and expected. Although it was very inconvenient for the family. Cleaning can happen any day!

I chose to break free from these unhealthy dynamics, seeking to cultivate a life of choice, equity, and freedom.

Overcoming the effects of living alongside poverty, domestic violence, chronic illness in my family, coupled with the hardships of migration, has made me tired of the way things have always been, stronger as a whole, humble and compassionate towards myself and others. I have learned to accept the parts of my past that caused me pain and transform that pain into fuel for my passion to help awaken others to their power in this life.

Growing up in the Dominican Republic, I grew up in two worlds: one of extreme poverty and making do with what you have and the other, having access and power. For me, it was a gift to be able to see both of these worlds. Both of my grandparents were entrepreneurs from my mother's side. My papa, Juan Antonio, whose nickname was Negro, sold eggs to local "colmados" (small stores). This venture was a family affair. I remember being part of the group encircling a big washing bucket where we repackaged the eggs for my grandfather's daily runs to sell to the local colmados. I loved helping out in this way; as a child, I thought it was the most incredible thing.

I never thought of my family or myself as poor, but by definition, they were. Looking back, I didn't realize at the time how many people slept in my grandmother's house. We all shared a very small house, less than 1200 square feet. It was a small three-bedroom house, and often, 13 to 14 adults and children were sleeping there.

On the other hand, my paternal grandfather was a successful business owner, shoemaker, and shoe designer with a big factory. He had many employees. One of my earliest memories with him was going to talk to each of his employees and asking them to make sure that they didn't waste my grandfather's materials and that they use his materials to the best of their ability.

Those early years before migrating to the United States with my parents and my three other siblings were a time when I learned about the dynamics of power, and financial freedom through entrepreneurship and envisioned a life bigger than what was presented to me.

THE LEARNINGS

I have faced many challenges on the road to becoming who I am today. Firstly, I learned that I had to be okay with being different from others around me. I can accept today that I'm not a bad person because I'm not always compliant with the status quo. While I used to feel ashamed at feeling different from my peers, I know now that standing out is one of my superpowers.

I also learned that I must care for my mental health continuously. I grew up in an environment of abuse and control, and it's important to me to break that cycle. Sometimes, these patterns are so hard-wired in us from an early age that we unconsciously create those environments in our adult lives as well, and I want better for my family. I show up with an open mind and heart, no matter what. As much as I humanly can, I am determined to provide my children with a better start so that they can go on to create healthy, fulfilling, and meaningful relationships.

I'll admit, I've been a lifelong people pleaser. I used to be the first to sacrifice my wants and needs for the sake of others. However, over the years, I've realized that I've twisted myself into knots and made myself miserable because of this programming of being an overgiver y "siempre a la orden" – no, thank you! This is not a sustainable plan for me; sometimes, I am unavailable. It's called boundaries!

Today, I continuously make space for my joy and happiness!

A huge life lesson came from being an immigrant to the US and finding my place by learning a new language, adjusting to the culture, and feeling a sense of belonging in this country. I learned people live differently in the US than what I was used to. Closed doors versus open doors was so striking to me. I learned that if I can make it here, I can make it anywhere. It was ingrained in me that I had to work twice as hard as everyone else to get ahead, which is something I have had to deprogram in myself. I also had to learn English quickly to help myself and my parents as their interpreter.

I have also found that the US is not what people imagine it is from outside its borders. I have often found myself discouraged by the challenges of being a woman of color in a country where systemic racism is so prevalent. Then I am fueled with hope through my clients and students who, through their courage to lead, to be better and different, are helping to shape a better world.

I've made it my mission to support other rising leaders like myself "mi gente", to awaken their power of choice, their power to co-create and live the life that they imagine, not just for themselves, but also to create conditions for their families also to thrive, to heal generational patterns.

I have found over the years that one of my biggest hurdles is overcoming my own limiting beliefs. I choose now to meet these beliefs head-on, examine them, and toss them aside as much as possible. I refuse to be the person who keeps me small today. I lean into my power and my assets and I encourage myself to reach for the stars as often as possible.

An ongoing practice of self-compassion and self-acceptance has helped me overcome these challenges. I have sought the help of a therapist, coaches, spiritual guidance, and a lot of books. My educational path has been non-traditional. I had the opportunity to be homeschooled at a young age allowing me to learn to read by the age of three. I also spent a lot of time with my parents at work, setting me on a path of experiential learning. I have always loved learning my way, so when I learned that I could create my major at Lesley University, I did just that. I designed a major that allowed me to study what I loved: human potential and doing business for good.

Over time, I have learned and continue to remind myself that I don't have to do any of this alone and that having support is the best way forward for me.

I also experienced a near-death experience in the form of a car accident that felt like a reset in my life and transformed the way I saw myself and my purpose for living. I was driving to one of my many gigs at the time on a rainy day. My car hit a bump on the road and fishtailed, sending my first brand new car spinning into a guard rail that protected me from entering the Charles River across from the Harvard University dorms. As my car was spinning, I saw my entire life flash before my eyes like a movie. After reviewing my entire life in what felt like an hour but was only seconds, I felt an immense sense of peace come over me as I surrendered my life and asked God to allow my family to be okay with my absence. I closed my eyes and was surprised to find myself in my body without an injury. It felt like I was given a second chance to live life on purpose.

Many days, what keeps me going is the love of my community, my own family, my biological family, and my purpose to help others awaken and support me in living my truth every day.

I feel that my very birth was a disruption of the established norms and family system that I was born into. I was told that as a baby, my screams made the walls vibrate. My birth changed my family forever as I was my mother's first child and my father's first daughter. Today, I operate in spaces where I am the only woman of color or one of very few. My very existence in these professional spaces is a disruption of white supremacy and the status quo. I hope to continue using my voice to make walls vibrate, shatter glass ceilings, and shake the earth for positive change that ripples through all humanity.

THE INSPIRATION

Growing up, I was inspired by the mysteries and magic of nature. As a child, I climbed trees and found a haven in them. I looked up at the vast expanse of the sky and was inspired by how expansive my life could be. I am still inspired by the sheer wonder of nature and all it gives us. I do my best to practice biomimicry, which is the science and art of emulating the processes of nature in all we do. One way that I learned to practice this is to remind myself that everything has its ebbs and flows – relationships, projects, and life in general – so I don't expect to be in perpetual harvest. There is a time to plant the seed, a time to water it, a time to watch it grow, a time to pluck the fruit, and then do it all over again.

I also learned that as a woman, I go through these stages of Winter, Spring, Summer, and Fall myself every month. As women, our energy levels fluctuate depending on the time of the month we are in. For example, our energy is low in our Winter week (the week we are menstruating). We start feeling our energy return the following week as we enter the Spring. Our energy peaks the following week in our Summer week and starts to wane the following week in our Fall week. Knowing this predictable energetic cycle allows me to plan my month to do my best work when I feel the most energy and to have absolute grace and care for myself in the weeks when energy is decreased. This has been so liberating for me and other women I coach because it has allowed us to be free of the idea that we must be on and perfectly producing 100 percent of the time.

Some of my biggest inspirations in my life have been the women who came before me. My mother Digna is a peaceful and gentle soul. I carry with me the legacy of my grandmother, Dolores whose resolve, generosity, and care for others inspire me to want to uplift all of humanity. My Godmother Ramona instilled in me the belief that I could become important and help others like her.

I often share about the power of the written word to inspire the world. I'm an avid reader and writer, and I've found that both of those hobbies expand my world and my thinking in ways that surprise me even to this day. I highly recommend reading about a variety of topics, as much as you can get your hands on. You will be on a grand adventure without leaving your couch.

I'd love to share a list of books that inspired and shaped me as well:
1. Create Your Best Year, One Day at A Time, by ,me Clara Angelina Diaz
2. If Life is a Game, These are The Rules by Cherie Carter-Scott
3. Practical Intuition by Laura Day
4. The Power of Now by Eckhart Tolle
5. A New Earth by Eckhart Tolle
6. Way of the Peaceful Warrior by Dan Millman
7. Ask and It's Given by Esther and Jerry Hicks

When I'm processing feelings or when I have something I feel compelled to share, the first thing I do is pick up a pen and paper. I've found writing to lead me to inspired choices and it frees me from heavy feelings. There is so much healing that can be done by writing. I've often found sparks of inspiration or solutions to my problems just by writing them out. Writing "Create Your Best Year, One Day at a Time" was like creating a guide for myself. It's a reminder that every day holds the potential to make the best days of my life, forever and always.

THE ADVICE

Looking back at my younger self, I would tell her: "Do everything in your power to become your own best friend mentally, physically, and spiritually. Many people can attempt to hurt, abandon, discount, and forget you, but you must not do that to yourself. Work on cultivating the voice of the wise and compassionate adult within."

For me, the biggest shift in my mindset was the practice of being 100 percent responsible for myself. From that place, I can receive more freely from others what they are willing to give. I no longer need to contort myself into any version of myself that I think they want me to be. I can own myself, my actions, and my decisions fully and completely.

For those of you who tend toward people-pleasing, this isn't an easy lesson to learn or an easy thing to practice. So many of us get uncomfortable when saying the word no or not conforming to meet other people's expectations. My advice is to practice. Practice saying no or being your authentic self and see what happens. It gets a little easier each time, I promise.

In that same vein, through a lot of therapy and practice, I have also learned to speak my true feelings despite fearing judgment. My goal is to be free and speak up, even when others choose to stay silent. Give yourself permission to have a voice and use that voice!

I also recommend creating practices that support you on a spiritual and emotional level. My favorite practices that I employ to support myself are meditation, contemplation, reflection, reframing, and asking for help early and often! Finding that inner stillness, thinking carefully about my actions and reactions, giving myself a break, detaching from a story that's holding me back, writing a new narrative, and enlisting a support team are all game changers in how I operate in the world.

When I think about the advice I would most want to impart to a young person trying to find their way, I would say it's important to be honest about what you need in all areas of your life. You are important, and you deserve love and support, just like any other human. Decide what areas of your life you want to focus on and start pouring your energy there. You will be surprised by what grows from just giving attention to those areas of your life!

THE PATH FORWARD

You are powerful. You are so powerful that you create worlds and can co-create your reality. Get to know that power and get intimate with it. ! There are so many ways to do this! Spirituality, psychology, astrology, human design, therapy, mentoring, coaching and self-reflection have been my tools to know that I am a daughter of the Universe. Invest the necessary time to know yourself and live the highest version of who you are meant to be.

Educate yourself about yourself, the ways of this world, and the difference you want to make in it so that you can use your power effectively and responsibly. Do this to Lead and Liberate throughout your short trip on this earth.

You can be a co-creator of your life through a deep understanding and merging of who you are, who you want to be, and who you are called to become. Understanding yourself deeply will support you in becoming the leader you are meant to be.

ABOUT CLARA

A certified Master Coach for over 15 years, Clara Angelina Diaz-Anderson teaches Authentic and Executive Leadership Coaching at Harvard University School of Professional Development and Executive Education.

Clara is the founder of ClaraFying Coaching and Consulting Institute, a leadership development, executive coaching and consulting firm, where her team of coaches and consultants, lead culture transformation projects for a premier clientele that includes the City of Boston. Through culture assessments, analysis, and recommendations that include executive, career, and life coaching, DEIB consulting, organizational program creation, implementation and facilitation.

The institute also offers bilingual coaching, coaching certification training, leadership development courses, business advising, public speaking and custom-made workshops. As a multi-sector professional Clara has worked with historical local officials like the 1st Dominican Boston City Councilor Julia Mejía and the first Capeverdean State Representative and State Senator Liz Miranda. Harvard Business School recruited Clara to teach, coach, facilitate, and monitor their inaugural Interpersonal Dynamic Lab for their 1st year MBA students. In addition to working with some of the best in their field, her dream is to contribute to building a world where love, dignity, equity and compassion are the norm and not the exception.

Clara is originally from the Dominican Republic, and identifies as afro-caribeña. Her mission is to help humanity awaken to their innate power. She is a published author of the book "Create Your Best Year One Day At A Time". She lives in a suburb of Massachusetts with her two children and husband.

Learn more and connect with Clara at:
Website: https://www.clarafying.com/
LinkedIn: https://www.linkedin.com/in/clarafying/
Email: clara.coaching.certification@gmail.com

DULCE OROZCO

"Truly embracing our uniqueness, the combination of our personal experiences, talents, and perspectives that make us who we are, is magical.."

-    Dulce Orozco

~ ~ ~

Dulce Orozco is a Latina Immigrant Therapist and speaker; she is a Licensed Mental Health Counselor in the State of Massachusetts. Dulce's why is love, she wants her daughters, everyone she works with, and everyone on planet Earth to spend more time living in love than living in fear. Dulce's work has been recognized at Promoting Good's Event: Our Day of Good, and she was one of the Amplify Latinx 2023 Honoree Advancing Latina Leaders.

~ ~ ~

Para Julia y Elena: Nunca se les olvide la magia que llevan por dentro.

EMBRACING YOUR MAGIC:
A JOURNEY OF SELF-COMPASSION AND FLEXIBILITY

THE JOURNEY

Thank you for reading my story. Before we start, is there anything you can do to make yourself more comfortable? Never underestimate the power of small movements. Now we are ready:

Am I a changemaker? Aren't we all?

It takes great effort for me to focus on what I've done instead of what I still have to do. It takes effort for me to feel I am doing enough. From my work as a therapist, I have the gift of closely seeing how we constantly change and create change in the world around us. The word 'changemaker' by itself isn't as powerful as it may be to some since, in my opinion, we are all changemakers. Instead, I look further and ask myself:

What kind of changemaker do I want to be? What type of change do I want to co-create?

I was a more confident person when I was younger, but that changed somewhere along the journey. It happened after I came to the United States when I was 17, idealizing everything here, and became a follower. I tended not to question things, even if they didn't feel right, because I felt like I had no right to complain when, back home in Venezuela, my family was struggling with so many things.

As I grew older, however, I learned the practice of tapping into the parts of myself that I trusted in order to create change. Once I could do that, I found the courage to speak up when something was wrong, even if it felt intimidating. I am still reclaiming those parts of myself, which has helped me embrace the journey of being the changemaker I want to be.

I was born in 1983 in San Cristobal, Venezuela, on Colombia's border. Living an hour away from Colombia at a time when the Colombian Guerrilla was so active was very challenging. My grandfather was a rancher, and owning land put him and his family at risk of being kidnapped, even though my parents were middle-class University Professors. Growing up seeing people I knew being kidnapped, including family members and children who went to my school, was terrifying and shaped the way I see the world.

A few things come to mind when I think about my biggest turning points. Coming to the United States at such a young age and seeing how the situation in Venezuela declined so drastically while my whole family was still living there affected me deeply on a profound level. Meeting my husband and finding a life partner who believed in me and what I do has shaped my life in immeasurable ways. Even though I consider myself adventurous, he always encourages me to do that thing that feels too big. Becoming a mom may have been one of my life's most significant turning points. My life changed completely because I wanted to show my daughters that it is possible to live in a different way. The pandemic and everything that happened during it and because of it changed my worldview. During that time, I realized I was spending more time living in fear than living in love, and I wanted to change that.

My default is to have almost unreachable expectations from myself. Realizing this, I have done a lot of intentional work to change that mindset and to remind myself that I can choose a more loving way to do things. All those times that I considered "failures" in the past were a necessary part of my learning process. At the same time, I learned that how I was relating to myself and my "failures" and high expectations was not sustainable and only left me feeling awful about myself.

Growing up in Venezuela, where mental health was not a priority, and seeing people very close to me dying or barely surviving suicide attempts made me curious about what we could do differently.

I am the oldest of four daughters, and my sisters are triplets. My parents and extended family did their best to prevent me from feeling left out after they were born; however, it was not until many years later that I realized that I had taken it upon myself to be the best I could be so that my parents wouldn't have to worry about me. I may have taken this a little too far, and the result was being hyper-independent, wanting to do everything by myself with little help from others. Asking for help is challenging for me, and interestingly enough, it is one of the things I most often see in my work with people from immigrant families and Latinas.

As a psychology student, all I wanted to do was work in clinical therapy. Knowing very little about the higher education system in the United States, the routes and options were very confusing. It took me a long time to do it, but I finally became a Licensed Mental Health Counselor.

This profession does not exist in Latin American countries; there are only Psychologists. In the US, however, psychologists aren't the only ones qualified to provide clinical therapy. Social workers and Licenced Mental Health Counselors like me are also able to serve in this way. Many friends, family members, and clients referred to me as Dulce "la psicologa" for the longest time, which made me feel like an imposter. I'd say, "Please don't call me that. I have a Master's and a CAGS (Certificate of Advanced Education Studies) but don't have a Ph.D...Therefore, I don't deserve that title."

It took me years to recognize that the translation of what I do here with one title has another title in other countries. I still correct them when this happens, but it no longer comes from a place of shame, but a place of love and admiration for all the amazing Latinas with a Ph.D. while remembering that I am enough as I am.

I worked in a world-renowned psychiatric hospital for a year, hoping they would give me a work visa; however, that didn't happen. I decided to follow the path many Licensed Mental Health Counselors had navigated before me and began working at community health centers. While in the hospital, I spoke Spanish only once. However, in the community mental health arena, I had the opportunity to speak Spanish daily. Using my background in a culturally humble way was very much needed and appreciated.

Even though I did not know it then, I soon found myself in burnout. It was no longer financially or emotionally sustainable to meet productivity standards, constantly solve crises, and work with highly traumatized people. As a family and without outside support, we decided I would take a leap of faith and start my own practice. Having children now, my husband and I felt this was the best way for us to orchestrate childcare while balancing our careers.

Seven years, one global pandemic, and another child later, I have a thriving business called Latina Immigrant Therapist LLC. I have since learned that I can do much more than 1:1 therapy. Luckily, my job combines my skills and talents with my passion: helping Latinx people and people from immigrant families. I also began working with companies offering wellness workshops, and I've also had success as a speaker. I have had the opportunity to collaborate with businesses for corporate retreats and have also served as a consultant to nurture mental health culture. I have even worked with college students and other amazing organizations to support Latinx adolescents.

I am excited to continue to discover new possibilities that ignite the spark in my heart, and I am entirely sure that this was possible because of the support and help I have gotten not only from my family but from my fantastic network of other extraordinary Latinas willing and open to share their knowledge, and magic with me.

THE LEARNINGS

I have learned so much from my life experiences. I am lucky to have a career that taught me to self-reflect, and I encourage myself, as I encourage others I work with, to pay careful attention to my own mindset and inner narrative. Words are so powerful, and we underestimate that.

Guilt and I have a very close relationship. I now know that the guilt won't go away on its own and that the more I try to resist it, the more it persists. As cliché as it sounds, what can happen when we can truly accept things as they are is unbelievable.

Becoming a therapist was challenging, mainly because of the immigration component, since I needed to be sponsored by a company. As grateful as I am to the organization that sponsored me, I experienced feeling undervalued and disrespected while simultaneously living with the fixed mindset of "I can't find anything better, and nobody else will sponsor me." This mindset kept me frozen longer than I needed to be.

The pandemic was pivotal for me. My husband worked at an international airport, so he continued to work while the rest of the world seemed to shut down. I lost people that were dear to me. Living in fear was, in and of itself, causing me to miss out on life.

My immediate family was always supportive; however, I did what many immigrants do: I stayed quiet. I chose not to share everything that had happened to me or how I was feeling. I kept telling myself that it was unfair for me to complain about my problems here with everything my loved ones were going through in Venezuela.

It took a lot of growth and self-reflection for me to begin to recognize that a fixed mindset tricks me into thinking that I don't have other options. I became determined to work to change that mindset, which resulted in me discovering more compassionate ways to find my inner strength.

Life often will teach me lessons through the beautiful people around me. My husband has always pushed me and encouraged me to try new things, which I appreciate with all my heart. I have also learned new perspectives by having therapy with a Latina Immigrant therapist like myself, who helped me process my life experiences and my feelings. It is very important for me to clarify that I was lucky to find the RIGHT therapist for me at that time, which is key in any therapeutic journey. Of course, I also had a few friends that I could talk to. However, the reality is that I was still operating under the mentality that I needed to figure out things on my own, so I kept myself closed off from their help until I started working with a therapist of my own.

I am still learning to ask for help. I am much better at it because it's a practice that I continue on an ongoing basis. I have built a supportive network among friends and am invested in working with excellent therapists and coaches who are part of my support system.

After coming to the United States, a part of me felt afraid of challenging the status quo. However, I have learned that I am already doing that every day just by being here. I can find examples of this in my everyday life, like being a Latina immigrant who charges a premium fee. I also choose not to speak English in our home (even though I have to repeat "Español o Portugués Por favor" several times daily to remind my children). I helped my seven-year-old daughter create a school project about Shakira as her famous historical person, and I correct people today when they pronounce my name wrong. I am creating a space for myself and other Latinx folks like me here in this country.

In my work, I try to co-create spaces where the status quo is challenged in more significant ways. I work with individuals and families to process their journey and to create their own paths. It's a beautiful career, and I feel so lucky to be a part of these powerful spaces.

I have learned that my life is better when I remember that I am not alone, can ask for help, and have the power to look for spaces that feel better and more aligned with what I want and need. And I hope that through my work, I can also offer others these reminders, inspiration, and safe spaces.

THE INSPIRATION

I have been lucky enough to find inspiration in plenty of places!

My daughters are my biggest inspiration. Knowing that I have the gift and responsibility of being an example to them is both scary and exciting. My hope is to show them how things can be different and how they can create their own reality. I am able to find the motivation to be and do better because of them.

As a student, I don't remember hearing about the importance of having mentors and sponsors; I am not sure if it was because I was not exposed to it being an international student or if that was not as common back then. However, I was blessed to have the best supervisor in my first grad school internship, who became my lifelong mentor, friend, and chosen family. Later on, I intentionally looked for mentors, and one of them recently told me something I try to practice daily. She said, "Dulce, don't be afraid to ask for what you need." It sounds simple, right? And yet, it can be challenging for many of us.

Working in private practice can be lonely if I don't intentionally look for spaces to interact and create community. This is why I chose to build a community of support and like-minded people. I made it my mission to plug into powerful spaces and seek out that connection.

What we can find when we look for it is fantastic. Professionally, I wanted to change how I worked for years and felt brave enough to do it once I joined a group of like-minded therapists working to transform their mindsets and relationships with money. In many ways, the pandemic played a significant role in bringing together global communities of individuals with shared interests and experiences.

Spirituality and energetic work have also been essential parts of my journey. I have been lucky enough to find excellent teachers and mentors in Latin America who have been instrumental in my process. Connecting to this part of myself in Spanish feels better and easier.

I remember reading the first Extraordinary Latinas book and reaching out to some of the women I learned about from the book. That resulted in beautiful friendships and deep inspiration, so I feel honored to be included in this book volume.

I have intentionally invested a lot of my time and energy in networking and meeting beautiful, inspiring, encouraging, supportive, and brilliant people, many of whom I consider great friends. I have been called a "great connector," which is a beautiful compliment since introducing people who inspire me is always very exciting. It is hard to describe how I feel when I write an email introducing two incredible people and telling them why I thought they needed to learn about each other.

I started listening to podcasts during the pandemic, and I LOVE them. There are so many podcasts by wonderful Latinas that inspire me. Podcasts have been a great way to learn about people doing work I love and deeply admire. I have reached out to many people I have met through podcasts and connected in ways I couldn't imagine.

One thing I love about finding these inspirations is how they organically multiply since, usually through my connections, I find out about more extraordinary people doing beautiful work. A coach I worked with who is now a great friend taught me the importance of telling the people who inspired you how you feel about them. I LOVE this practice, especially among the Latinx community. We grow together when we tell others how they've helped us and how their teachings and experiences impacted us. After all, it takes all of us, as one of my favorite t-shirts says. People who are passionate about what they do for the greater good and want to share it with others inspire me because their passion is contagious.

THE ADVICE
Treat Yourself Well

When I think about what I'd done differently throughout my life thus far, I find myself wishing I had treated myself better. My default was to be self-critical and to underestimate what I had accomplished. I have invested time, energy, and money to change this and have learned to relate to myself more lovingly and compassionately. Something very helpful for me throughout this process has been to expand my capacity to be flexible and look for other options and alternative ways.

Practice Loving Flexibility

Practicing loving flexibility helped me see that instead of choosing one way or the other, which caused a lot of internal conflict, I could accept both as a part of me because, after all, I am a complex being, which is okay. That is how I learned something I remember daily: I can be grateful and still want better things for myself and my family. I used to live feeling like an ungrateful person. Why would I want more than I already had? My guilt felt stronger whenever I wanted something better since I already had so much, especially living in a country with more opportunities than my home country. Now I know that I can be grateful for what I have, AND I can also want better opportunities that continue to evolve with me.

Practicing flexibility also means intentionally changing some of the words I use to describe myself and looking for reframes that make me feel more integrity. In my therapeutic work, this is one of the things I do the most. Words are potent, and many words we use to describe ourselves are passed on to us and learned. Reframes may take some labels and weight off. So instead of saying: "I am horrible at budgeting," I can start telling myself: "I am learning new ways to do this that feel better and easier to me."

Ask for Help

Asking for help is also a way to expand my capacity to be flexible. It used to seem "easier" for me to find ways to do everything myself until I realized the price I was paying. I could get extremely tired or overwhelmed since there was no way I could do everything, or I could get irritable because I felt things weren't the way I wanted them to be. Even though it feels more accessible now because I have practiced asking for help, it takes flexibility to recognize when I have reached the point where I need to ask for help. I am proud to say that because of this ability to ask for help, I have been able to work with amazing people supporting my growth and development process. Paying for their services and help has been an excellent investment in myself and my work.

Finding flexibility in little things ultimately adds up and creates more space to look at things differently. Ask yourself what else could be possible? It is a way to work your flexibility muscle, which can help you be nicer with yourself.

Practice Self Compassion

Self-compassion has been life-changing for me. Many times, the response I get from the people I work with when we start talking about self-compassion is that it sounds great, but it must take a lot of time and effort. However, that does not have to be the case. Simply asking yourself, "What do I need right now?" can be a way to start practicing self-compassion.

Be In Your Body and Stay Present

As humans, we spend most of our time revisiting the past or worrying about the future, so being present can feel very challenging. I have learned that my senses help me be more present. If I can focus on what I'm seeing, feeling, hearing, smelling, and touching, I can be more in the here and now. I find that I feel the most present when I am doing what I want to do, such as watching my daughters play.

Spirituality and energy work also help me to be nicer to myself and to treat myself better. Believing in something bigger than myself and connecting to it when needed is very powerful.

Treating myself more lovingly and compassionately and expanding my capacity to be flexible resulted in finding a new way to connect with my worth. It is exhausting not to feel enough. Instead, I choose to embrace my uniqueness, which reminds me that I am, in fact, worthy of all the wonderful things this life has brought me. This applies not only to me, but also to all of us. We are all unique, and our uniqueness is magical since nobody else can do things the way each of us can. This has become one of the main pillars of my work with Latinxs and people of color.

THE PATH FORWARD

Embrace your uniqueness. Can you imagine how different the world would be if we all did this? Especially among Latinx in the United States, where, unfortunately, because of previous history, there is still a lot of scarcity mindset and competition among us.

The combination of our personal experiences, talents, and perspectives that make us who we are is magical. It leaves no space for us to feel worthless, less than, or the dreaded imposter syndrome. When we remember and learn ways to see our gifts and what we can offer to the world that nobody else can, all the energy spent worrying can instead be used to find new ways to share our gifts with the world.

By embracing your uniqueness, fantastic and magical collaborations can happen more organically since it can be easier to recognize not only your own gifts but also the gifts of others. Therefore, supporting and valuing one another, especially as Latinx, can be done lovingly and respectfully.

Remember to replace the OR with the AND; you are more than one thing! It does not have to be this OR that; it can be this AND that. Add as many ANDs as needed, and be okay with changing them because you are constantly changing.

And lastly, you don't have to do it all by yourself, even if you are great at it. Ask for help; it may be from a therapist, cleaning services, a coach, a personal trainer, or a friend. Asking for help is not a sign of weakness but a sign of self-love. Consider the positive impact this has on those you love, showing them the importance of prioritizing well-being.

ABOUT DULCE

Dulce Orozco is a Latina Immigrant Therapist and speaker; she is a Licensed Mental Health Counselor in the State of Massachusetts. Dulce's why is love, she wants her daughters, everyone she works with, and everyone on planet Earth to spend more time living in love than living in fear.

She loves to co-create safe spaces where we can thank fear and explain that we don't need it at this time, so we can give ourselves the chance to see new alternatives. Because of her personal and professional experience working in private practice, community mental health, psychiatric hospitals, and counseling centers, she is fascinated by culture's role in mental health and how we perceive ourselves. As a result, she creates safe spaces to talk about complicated but critical topics. She has presented at Google, Association of Latino Professionals for America, Merrimack College, The City of Cambridge, Love your Magic, GitLab, and Amundi, among other places. Dulce's first language is Spanish, and she is also fluent in English and Portuguese.

Dulce's work has been recognized at Promoting Good's Event: Our Day of Good, and she was one of the Amplify Latinx 2023 Honoree Advancing Latina Leaders.

Dulce was born and raised in Venezuela and has lived in Massachusetts since 2001. She has two young daughters who constantly remind her how to enjoy the present, prioritizing play. She loves being a student and is usually learning something new.

Learn more and connect with Dulce at:
https://www.dulceorozco.com/
https://www.linkedin.com/in/latinaimmigranttherapist/
https://www.instagram.com/latinaimmigranttherapist/

GRISELDA ABOUSLEMAN

"Obstacles in life are inevitable, and the most important aspect of learning and using this adversity to our advantage is in the choices we make to overcome them"

- Griselda Abousleman

~ ~ ~

With a degree in Industrial Engineering from Stanford University and an MBA from Arizona State University, Griselda built a remarkable career in Corporate America as an Operations Executive and Continuous Improvement leader. She was previously a Board Chair for the Women in Manufacturing Association whose mission is to support, promote, and inspire women in the manufacturing industry. Today, Griselda's passion for empowering others led her to establish Lean Business Excellence, a consulting business focused on business advising and leadership coaching.

~ ~ ~

I dedicate this book to my Nenita. That's the nickname I have for my dear mother who persevered so much to bring us the fulfilling life my siblings and I enjoy today. This chapter is a short summary of my book, Life Beyond the Border: A Journey from Poverty to Passionate Purpose. In sharing our story, I hope to ignite the passion in everyone out there to pursue their purpose with passion, and bring their heroes along with them. In my case, my mom.

EMPOWERED RESILIENCE: TRANSFORMING ADVERSITY INTO STRENGTH AND PASSION

THE JOURNEY

Life is truly a journey of unexpected surprises. All of us get punched in the gut with challenging events and adversity at some point in our lives, and many times, when least expected. I'm here to tell you that we should be thankful for these experiences, and through this chapter, I'm hopeful you'll understand what I mean.

My journey starts on the meandering Rio Grande River along the South Texas/Mexico border in a lively city called Brownsville, Texas. That's where I was born and raised with my sister, two brothers, and my hard-working parents, who immigrated to the United States after they married in April 1970. Before I tell you about my journey, it is important to understand my background and the strong women that made a significant impact in my life.

Beatriz Cortez Montejano was my maternal grandmother. She was a lady who lived through many challenges in life, gave birth to her children at home, and had the heartbreaking misfortune of burying three of her ten children. She was not a woman to dwell on her misfortunes, though. She was resourceful and found solutions to all obstacles in front of her. She practically raised her children independently, as my grandfather was a talented musician who wasn't always around to help. Through her amazing journey of hard work, devotion to her children, and perseverance, Beatriz ensured that her surviving children had a happy and healthy life: this required sacrifice and resourcefulness. For example, she taught her three older daughters how to clean homes, iron, and encouraged them to learn a skill like hairstyling.

Unfortunately, it also meant that they had to put these skills to work at a young age, and they were each pulled out of school during their elementary school years. As young dropouts, her daughters, Isaura, Magdalena, and Sandra (my mom), managed to work their way through their teenage years to provide the means for the four younger ones to complete school and get an education.

My mother is a resilient and beautiful woman with a charming personality. As a young girl, she worked hard to ensure that my grandmother had her own sewing machine for her sewing jobs and so that her siblings had what they needed to achieve some college-level study. This all happened before she turned sixteen, which is when she married my father, who was 24 and living in Brownsville, Texas. My Dad's father was also living in Brownsville, while my mom was trying to make ends meet in Matamoros, a bordering city in Mexico, where both my parents were born.

My mom had never planned on leaving Mexico, but when she met my dad and fell in love, she soon found herself a teenager in a new country with a young daughter (my older sister) in her arms. They were living in the United States with only hope and prayer on their side. Then, without much access to medical advice or means, just sixteen months later, she gave birth to me. There we were, three young girls: an infant, a toddler, and their teenage mother, trying to make ends meet in a new place where everything seemed so foreign to them. Fortunately, we had each other and my Dad, one of the most loving and caring men I have ever met.

Like my older sister, Sandra, I was born on a hardwood floor at a midwife's home on Jackson Street in Brownsville, Texas, just a few blocks from my grandfather's home. I was a surprise present for my parents – or at least I'd consider myself a lovely gift! As a young couple in a new country, my Mom admits I was more of a humble unexpected accident who was almost two pounds heavier than my older sister. After the initial shock that I was not the boy they were hoping for and also much larger than her last baby, dad convinced mom that having a robust healthy baby girl was a good thing. She eventually agreed, of course, but I can only imagine that being so young and having two young children in a new country was probably an overwhelming experience.

Growing up in Texas was a fun adventure for my sister and me. We enjoyed memorable family times living in a small home built by Dad in my grandparents' backyard. Our small home had everything we needed, and we had each other. The best part was that we were also a few steps from our grandmother, whom we loved dearly. She was a loving and caring lady who always had our best interests at heart.

These are the role models that shaped my humble beginnings and I couldn't be more proud to come from such amazing people.

THE LEARNINGS

I have had plenty of pivotal moments in my life, and I can honestly say today that I am sincerely grateful for every single one of them. The first was when my sister and I entered Longoria Elementary School speaking Spanish and were forced to learn English through full immersion. It was a challenge that we happily accepted and we enjoyed everything that school life had to offer.

My Mom and Dad had solid jobs for some time but did have to adjust when my mother experienced her first layoff from the Atari company during the Atari shock of 1983. The video game market crashed, and Atari lost more than $350 million dollars and laid off more than one-third of its staff during this period.

Our family had to navigate living on a single income after the massive layoffs, which impacted not only my mom, but also the parents of many of our school friends. Our family and our community came together, and we persevered. While I'd always had a close family unit, it was the first time I understood the power of a close-knit community and how we can care for one another.

Around that time, Mom and Dad also added two additional brothers to our little crew. My first brother was planned and expected. His name was Lucio José Castro, after my father. An amusing note here is that my sister Sandra's full name was Sandra Lucila Castro, in honor of both mom's and dad's names – Sandra and Lucio. Funny enough, us unplanned children, my youngest brother and I, never received a middle name. We were just Griselda and Emmanuel. We love to tease our parents about this.

Another pivotal moment in my life was my younger brother's severe illness. When he was a toddler, Lucio was hospitalized for weeks due to a severe infection. The doctors offered minimal hope for his survival. However, through collective prayers from extended family members and our community, my brother miraculously pulled through. Witnessing the constant stream of visitors during his hospitalization was scary, as it made us understand the seriousness of his condition. For several weeks, we stayed in my grandmother's home as my parents spent numerous nights at the hospital. Throughout this challenging period, the strength of family unity and the power of prayer played crucial roles in helping us navigate that stressful time.

While my high school years created some beautiful memories, they also brought new obstacles. One of these that I hold near and dear to my heart was our district's rejection of our funding request when we asked for money to start an advanced placement (AP) program at our school. Fire ignited in my gut when I heard the reasoning – they thought our students couldn't pass this test; therefore, it was considered a waste of money. That was enough for me to gather as many students as I could and work to prove them wrong. Fortunately, we also had some caring teachers who helped us learn these AP strategies without pay. They volunteered their time and even weekends to teach us calculus, physics, and world history. Through perseverance, hard work, and sheer will to prove them wrong, our senior class came through! Several of us scored 3s, 4s, and 5s to get an advanced placement curriculum started at Gladys Porter High School! Life was good and again, I saw the power of a dedicated community and sheer determination led to triumph!

These events reinforced my character and taught me never to give up. I did need some reassurance and gentle nudges at times, though. For example, the day I got admitted to Stanford was a challenging one for me. I was set on enrolling at nearby Rice University, but my mother had different plans for me. When I received my acceptance letter to Stanford University with a full scholarship and financial aid, she insisted I head out to California instead. Heartbroken and afraid, this young girl, who had never ventured out of the state of Texas other than to Matamoros to visit family, headed out to California. I wasn't sure what to expect, but I leaned into what I'd learned so far in life – that I could face obstacles, even when they seemed intimidating!

THE INSPIRATION

While at Stanford, I quickly learned that I was unprepared to excel at the rigorous academic requirements I encountered. My Spanglish language was my first obvious struggle. I had to focus and practice English and Spanish to have basic conversations and perform well in my classes. Then, I noticed I had to study about three times longer than my peers. I had not noticed how ill-prepared my high school education was until other high-performing valedictorians and students with impressive educational backgrounds surrounded me. I practiced speaking every chance I got and studied extensively with lots of help from professors, friends, and teaching assistants. After a lot of hard work, dedication, devotion to my studies, and with sincere appreciation to all those who helped me, I proudly received my Stanford Industrial Engineering degree in 1994.

During my years at Stanford, my parents were an invaluable support system and source of inspiration back home. They prepared and sold tamales every quarter to help me buy my college essentials and books. I also chose to study abroad for one quarter, and to pay for this, my parents ended up selling their home and moving into the Border Apartments in Brownsville.

The challenging moments continued into my adult years. These continued to shape my strong character and relentless determination to succeed against all odds. I married at the age of twenty-eight. As is common in Mexican customs and traditions, if a young girl is unmarried by age twenty-five, something must be wrong with her. I was exhausted by family questions during family weddings about when I was going to be next. Whether under pressure or not, I married, probably prematurely, and although that marriage only lasted five years, I did receive one of the most beautiful blessings from it – my daughter Briana was born when I was thirty years old.

Having a daughter inspired me in so many ways. Being a mother gave my life new meaning and purpose, and I was driven to succeed for her. I was a traveling career woman and a single mom and enjoyed my work life. There were many nights and days when Briana went to work with me. She even traveled with me on several business trips. I had a career and a daughter; both responsibilities were extremely important to me. People at work talked about work-life balance. Briana was my balance, and my work was my fun, so I was perfectly balanced in my world. I kept thinking about what my dear child would actually remember years later and what impact this would have on her. I will mention that later in this chapter. I think you will be surprised.

Another source of inspiration in my life was love and the desire for it. Needless to say, I knew I was not meant to be alone. Having married previously for the wrong reasons, I felt that the most important decision in my life was who to choose as my lifelong partner. I had a daughter, a thriving career requiring much travel, and a desire for more children. There was an emptiness in my heart that I wanted to fulfill. How was that going to be possible?

My grandmother's resourcefulness instincts kicked in, and I signed up for Match.com. That's where I found my wonderful husband of sixteen years, Greg Abousleman. The dating site did everything for me; all I had to do was show up. We married less than a year after meeting and started a wonderful life together – just the three of us. Greg and I were clear on our goals and aspirations before we decided to unite our lives. I was a traveling career woman, and he was a businessman who preferred to live in New Mexico to lead the family's real estate and hardware retail business. We made a great team!

Our life was perfect for a while until we struggled to conceive a child of our own. We were heartbroken but determined not to give up. I just knew that the love in my heart was meant for more children, and I held on to that love as we navigated the emotional rollercoaster over the next few years. We experienced one loss after another, four in all, counting the last one at almost 12 weeks gestation. While the pain was heart-wrenching, I was inspired by the love I had for my daughter and my husband, and I knew I could get through it somehow.

We met several fertility specialists, and after years of struggling, our miracle baby, Gabriela María, was born on New Year's Eve 2009. This blue-eyed baby girl was a blessing to our lives! She has grown up to be an inquisitive teenager with a strong passion for math, science, and volleyball. Her creative thinking ability is far beyond what mine was at her age. She continually inspires me to keep my technical skills sharp and to never give up on the ever-changing facets of technology. She teaches me, challenges me, and continues to keep me on my toes with her strong determination to achieve whatever she sets her mind to. I continue experimenting and diving into social media, technology, and whatever else she thinks I need to avoid 'being left behind' as she calls it.

After Gabriela's birth, our challenges continued, as we were later blessed with a beautiful boy who we named Gregory. Our lives were turned upside down when he refused to eat shortly after being born. After testing, he was diagnosed with a chromosomal condition called Potocki-Lupski Syndrome, or PTLS for short. With the help of five therapists, nine doctors, and a much-needed g-tube in his belly, Gregory grew into a strong and charming boy, and his journey inspires me. I will forever claim that Greg and I were chosen to raise this dynamic duo, along with our energetic Briana, who was a tremendous help while I continued my travels for work.

My son Gregory inspires everyone who knows him to focus on the basic elements of life and happiness. To him, everything is good and kind. He enjoys warm hugs and has received several positivity awards for his never-ending optimism at school. To this day, every time we ask him for his Christmas wish list, his only response is, "My family, that's all I need for my life to be complete." He's a constant reminder that a simple smile and a hug do wonders for the heart and soul.

THE ADVICE

What I'd love to share with mothers as heartfelt advice is that children really do learn from what they see us do rather than what we tell them to do. You never know how the benefit of your hard work will inspire your own children. I mentioned earlier I would relay a surprising development about my strong daughter Briana. Well, that girl traveled with me to different places when I was a single mom. Her preschool, La Petite Academy, allowed me to take her to any academy nationwide, and my darling Briana became a social butterfly mingling with children from different states.

In her teen years, the more I told her what she should do, the less she seemed to listen. I often experienced guilt about my travels and how they'd affected her. Imagine my sincere surprise when I read Briana's college entrance essay. In short, she wrote what a positive impact I had on her as she watched me dive into my traveling career with vigor and joy. She was proud that she grew up helping her stepdad with the little ones, and she treasured the moments that we could spend together. She used these life lessons to develop her dedicated work ethic. So, to all those moms out there filled with guilt, let it go. What they see is what they learn, so keep doing it! You're serving them well.

Another piece of advice I'd share with you is that your lifelong partner is the most important decision you will make in life. This, I believe, is true for many reasons. In my case, I needed someone who was well-aligned with my career intentions and ambitions. I was an intelligent career woman, and I wanted to continue advancing in my career. Not every man is willing to support such an endeavor. Greg did this with pride and joy. He genuinely enjoyed watching me, his daughters, and other women do well in their business lives or careers. He had his own engineering career and saw the challenges other women faced in this male-dominated environment. He also appreciated the strong dedication and technical aptitude that women brought to the team, along with many of his male colleagues. He takes great pride in assisting women on his team advance and take on leadership roles. "I support and admire strong work ethic," he says, "and many times, I see this come through loud and clear through the hard-working women on our team."

Finally, a final piece of advice is to let your children inspire and challenge you. It's a bit daunting sometimes, as they tend to get wiser than you, or at least that's what they think or claim. I embrace that. They are stronger, smarter, and face life's challenges with a different attitude than we did. This enables them to embrace a strong growth mindset. It instills in them the perspective that they can accomplish anything in life and they educate mom or dad in many respects, whether it's with a charming personality, strong technical aptitude, or a simple love of life. There's always something to stay sharp on as we continue to mature in our lives.

THE PATH FORWARD

During this final section in my story of hope, courage, love, and turning adversity into advantages, I ask that you reflect on your own lives. I firmly believe that we each have a purpose in life and a story to share. My passion is to inspire others to find their purpose and pursue it with perseverance and determination. I get great satisfaction from helping others, whether people or businesses, to achieve objectives beyond what they thought was possible. There will be obstacles in life, guaranteed. Let those challenges propel you into greatness and strength.

I sincerely hope you know that there is help along the way and many people who care. As I capture my life's experiences here, hopefully you've realized that nothing is accomplished in solitude. There was help from people who cared, people who were ready to make an impact in someone else's life. At times, these angels or support systems may not be readily in front of you. It may mean that we have to look for them.

We have to reach out and find whatever help is needed at the time. You will find answers through people, resources, and, often, through self-reflection. I encourage you to reach out and let others propel you to the greater heights that you deserve. I would immensely enjoy comparing stories and helping you with your journey to excellence.

As I wrap up my story, in my own self-reflection, I know that I have grown tremendously through my many life experiences, the ups and downs and tribulations of life. I ask that you take the next step in identifying what excites you the most and pursue that passion with perseverance. As you do this, expect bumps, bruises, setbacks, mistakes, and many lessons learned. Know that we all have them. This, I believe, is what makes the mystery of life beautiful and intriguing all at once. You really never know what's coming next.

However, if you stay true to your passions, you will overcome adversity and prevail. These experiences will make you stronger, so embrace them. They are excellent opportunities that will enable you to conquer your fears and enable you to grow and move forward. In turn, I hope you also pay it forward and help another person, group, or organization. You're the hero of your own story! I encourage you to share it.

I end with one simple question for you: Are you ready to ignite your passion? Let's do this!

ABOUT GRISELDA

Griselda's personal and professional journey is truly inspiring. As a dedicated mother and wife, she finds joy in family life and takes pride in her children's achievements. Her background growing up in Brownsville, Texas, instilled in her the values of hard work, determination, and resilience, which she demonstrated through her education and career.

With a degree in Industrial Engineering from Stanford University and an MBA from Arizona State University, Griselda embarked on a remarkable career in Corporate America, where she honed her skills as an Operations Executive and Continuous Improvement leader. Her expertise in generating substantial savings for companies, leading cross-cultural teams, and implementing operational excellence frameworks speaks volumes about her abilities as a transformational leader.

Griselda's passion for empowering others led her to establish Lean Business Excellence, a consulting business focused on business advising and leadership coaching. Her dedication to helping people and businesses thrive is evident in her role as a coach, where she undoubtedly imparts her wealth of knowledge and experience to guide others toward success.

Griselda's authenticity, servant leadership, and ability to engage people in transformational change highlight her exceptional qualities as a leader. Her story serves as an inspiration not only to aspiring professionals but also to anyone striving to make a meaningful impact in their personal and professional lives.

Learn more and connect with Griselda at:

Email: griselda@businesscoachingresults.com
LinkedIn: www.linkedin.com/in/griselda-abousleman
Facebook: www.facebook.com/griselda.excellence
Instagram: www.instagram.com/theRealGriselda

IRENE QUEVEDO

"Latinas deserve to shine from within by taking up space in highly successful arenas. We deserve to get & stay big. The key to life is sustaining this elevated state of being to achieve prosperity."

Irene Quevedo

~ ~ ~

Irene is an established C-suite executive with 20+ years of experience in leadership & professional development. She is a successful author, public speaker, nonprofit leader, and executive coach. For fun she travels (a lot) and is a very proud momma of three teens! Irene's life is one of adventure, a little trial & error, and lots of love.

~ ~ ~

To my one & only daughter, Sofia. Continue to share your talents with the world, showing others how to stay true to their hearts, like you've always been true to yours.

EMBRACING IMPERFECTION: A JOURNEY TO SELF-ACCEPTANCE AND PROSPERITY

THE JOURNEY

I was born the youngest of six kids in a deeply Latino household. Unfortunately for me, I was born into a very dysfunctional family. Childhood made me strong - a fighter and hard worker. Therein lies the struggle of Latinidad. Even the strong need help, but I've struggled to ask for it my whole life. It took me forty-plus years on this planet to realize that asking for help is a superpower!

My three eldest siblings were left in Mexico when my mother came alone to the U.S., searching for the American dream. From the start, the three youngest siblings born in the U.S. were deemed "lucky." I was the baby of those three, which may lead one to believe that I was the luckiest and most prized child of all, but that's not my story. I was often left home alone with my older siblings, as my Mom worked a lot. My older siblings were abused and mirrored what they saw and went on to become abusers themselves. They turned out to be the ugliest part of my upbringing. Physical, sexual, and emotional abuse was as common as tortillas for dinner and church on Sundays. This isn't how our matriarch will remember it, and siblings 1-3 had such brutal battles to fight, so I spent much of childhood daydreaming about the future. I found my escape in school and saw it as my way out.

As a child, I learned to fend for myself and strived to be the perfect child, and like many first-generation Latinas, I was raised to think I wasn't perfect at all. My mother comes from a long line of guilt-tripping Catholic mothers who meant well, but broke us apart before we even had the chance to learn right from wrong. All of this contributed to who I am today because it set me on a path towards achievement that, at first, was meant to make my mother finally proud. However, I found that I'd never actually seem to make her proud. Instead, I found that I loved breaking the rules like a true diehard "baby of the family."

A major milestone for me was preschool. I got to attend early, wanting to follow my brother, who was 24 months older. I wasn't even potty trained yet. I'm told that I had to learn in a week in order to stay enrolled, and I succeeded. Even as a tiny child, I was motivated to stay in school!

I cherished my time in school. Everyone, including my siblings, praised my intelligence, and this positive reinforcement shaped my belief in my own abilities. With four out of five siblings unable to graduate high school, they poured their lost dreams into mine as I continued toward my goal of higher education. I knew going to college wasn't a guarantee, and I didn't take my chance for granted. I visited the University of California Santa Barbara as a freshman in high school and fell in love. For four years, I spoke my enrollment there into existence. I inherently believed in the concept of manifesting, even before I recognized it as such.

Before college graduation, I thought I'd maybe become a teacher or a lawyer. My first real job was as a camp counselor, where I learned that I love people, unifying them for greatness, working with their talent, and using this teamwork for good. It's no wonder I've always been in leadership roles – Captain of the cheer team, President of my sorority, and for many years now, CEO of a thriving organization.

I studied abroad in college, traveled to many countries as a student including Brazil, France, Italy, Spain and more, and formally studied abroad in Barbados. I received a dual Bachelor of Arts degree in Sociology and International Studies from UCSB. I also hold an MBA from Eastern University. I couldn't be more proud of how far I've come, and looking back, I realize that the determination and will to succeed came from the hardships of my younger life. I refused to stay in the cycle of poverty and abuse. I knew I had to leave and provide something different for my children.

Since I was an international studies major, my love of travel and yearning to learn about the globe led me to a lifelong journey and love affair with travel.

It is one of my greatest passions! It's a beautiful value that I've also instilled in my children. Their love of travel is healing a long history of trauma and turbulent generations of displacement. They get to reach out and have the best of life by learning that we are all connected in this world and need each other to improve it! They get to start by learning from their own cultural identity as Mexican/Guatemalan-Americans. Many times in college I'd say that I dreamed of raising global citizens, and twenty years later, I can proudly say I have. Again, manifested before I knew it.

THE LEARNINGS

Instead of making an imperfectly perfect parent proud, I fought for my life's goals and dreams by disrupting everything ever expected of me. When I went to college, travel became an obsession, and I recognized what a privilege it is. My mother traveled out of necessity, but here I am today, traveling for fun and as often as I can. This desire to explore the world was the first of many moments in my life where I'd felt misunderstood by my immigrant parents. My mother wanted me to sit still and stop doing what she perceived as "crazy," but I've found I actually love crazy. I always have and always will. I want to encourage other women to define their "crazy" and go after it, too!

Early in my career, I set out to succeed on my terms and stopped following the advice of people less successful than me or, in the case of my toxic family, unwilling to break generational curses. I went on to build not one, but three successful businesses. I became my company's first Latina and youngest CEO, but I did none of this by striving for perfection. I leaned into my superpower to ask those more successful than me for guidance, read business books, and believed in the power of manifestation. I wasn't ashamed to ask for support when needed, and it's that courage that I learned from my mother that brought me the highest monetary success of my life. This financial success led me to establish an executive coaching company, Wealthy Latinas. I was also successful at co-founding the Level Up Latina Podcast, a top-rated Latina podcast with over two hundred episodes currently streaming.

In the middle of a thriving C-suite career, I paused my professional life to go on a travel sabbatical, much to my family of origin's despair and judgment. But again, I wouldn't let dysfunctional individuals hold me back, and neither should you! Never give the broken that much power. I traveled the world with my children, ages 5, 6, and 11. I went on this magical journey with the person who's helped me most in this lifetime — my husband of almost two decades. I didn't know how our year abroad would unfold, but I knew I'd always have my voice. We named the journey Queventure, and you can travel along with us on Instagram (@queventure.abroad). Queventure was a pivotal moment in my young life as a mother, and it is where I developed the foundation for my thriving coaching business at WealthyLatinas.com. It is these seminal moments I wish every Latina would experience in their lifetimes.

THE INSPIRATION

As a child, my inspiration was to do well and finally feel seen by a family that made me feel invisible because, as the youngest, I had it "easy." In college, all I knew was hard work. I excelled. In marriage, I became the same - solid and dependable. But it all became problematic when I realized I didn't know why I desired achievement. I decided to stop chasing success for others and started doing it for myself. I began therapy, a game-changer, and I separated my finances from my husband's. From there, life prospered.

The books that helped me evolve include The House on Mango Street, Conversations with God, and Getting the Love You Want. These books are hugely different and were all uniquely powerful in my life.

I read the first, The House on Mango Street, in college. It was the first time I saw my family reflected in writing. I came home from college that first quarter and wanted to read it to my mother, who'd only had one year of schooling. I remember painting her toenails as I read. I know she was shocked by me at that moment. She looked perplexed at how college was changing me. I didn't get many moments like these in the remaining years of my university life. I grew vastly apart from the family. I came to recognize and learn so much about myself away from home, but I am grateful for that book and that moment that deeply rooted me in a home that I'd eventually seek to escape more than I'd return to for safety. That home was never a safe space for me, but it was the place for lessons, a place for learning to love my culture and develop Mexican pride. It was also the place that gave me all I needed to succeed, even if it wasn't easy to endure.

When I read Conversations with God, I felt God was there, removing all the guilt. I wanted to break away from my family's tired patterns of dysfunction, but I also felt terrible for wanting that. I loved and will always love my family of origin, but it would never be where I would grow, and knowing God loved me even if I distanced myself from all I ever knew made an impact.

Getting the Love You Want saved my marriage. Marriage is the hardest thing I've experienced; it's also my most precious accomplishment. This book and so many others helped transform me as a partner, and it helped that I have a husband who is as interested in healing, growing, and succeeding as I am. Marrying the right person in life is like a secret weapon, but that doesn't mean couples won't fight, change, and struggle. Working to get through marriage with faith and learning together is critical. It's so beautiful to think my husband and I built a family that, while imperfect, is also full of acceptance, guilt-free sentiments, and so much respect and love!

THE ADVICE

My younger self moved quickly into adulthood, perhaps too fast. As a first-generation college graduate, I assumed I needed to figure it all out. I was married, pregnant, buying a condo, and changing careers, all within 12 months in my mid-twenties. It was all too much, and as much as 20-somethings might feel they're running out of time, they're not! I wish my younger self would have slowed down and been more strategic. This is why I am a Life and Business Coach today, aside from being the Chief Executive Officer of a thriving community-based organization. More women need support from other women who've been successful so that we can learn from each other, but most critically, learn from our past failures.

In my late 20s, I was desperate for an entry-level job. Between 26 and 29, I had made so many financial and emotional mistakes, and with a toddler, I had to shift, or I'd lose it all....marriage, family, and, at times, what felt like my sanity. During these years, I'd moved so quickly that I neglected myself. I didn't turn to friends or family, which was another huge mistake. I was failing, but somehow, I wanted to fail in secret.

So please mark my words: DON'T GO AT IT ALONE! Seek out the help of those you admire, hire a coach, find a mentor, and ask for help in the form of moral support, accountability, or simply understanding. We need so much compassion on the journey to transforming for good. As we end generational patterns by facing generational traumas, we Latinas must stick together instead of falling apart, solas!

I turned my life around by surrounding myself with positive influences and mothers I respected. I started a mommy blog with a dear friend from college (for me, the precursor to co-founding Level Up Latina and my own company, Wealthy Latinas). I found blog writing to be therapeutic. My husband was my biggest cheerleader, and we saw my career as an investment as I grew that entry-level role from my late 20's to C-suite status in five short years! I did this by one, believing I deserved it, and two, by asking for help, and three, by leaning on others. Relying on others and finding success as a team led to the eventual success of establishing the Level Up Latina podcast with two of my closest friends. We would not have succeeded without each other, which is truly beautiful.

However, before there is a community, there is you. Your life is yours and yours alone. You may never get your parents to understand that, or maybe your friends from youth, or even at times, the spouse you love. Understanding, while beautiful, may never come from the outside, so find it deep inside of you. My mother's approval, for instance, escaped me in my 20s and 30s, and by all accounts, I was a success. Ironically, I'd learned how to be successful following her example of hard work and grit. She believes home ownership and a Mercedes are symbols of success. I wish being happy was the symbol; being a world traveler, marrying your best friend, raising exceptional children, living in a gorgeous home and neighborhood, and working hard would be it. Still, it never was, so I let go of the idea of gaining her approval. I've lived an extraordinary life, but I really started living it when I stopped expecting those I love to "get me."

I went on a magical journey of living for myself. I traveled nonstop in Latin America and the Caribbean for an entire year with my small children, visiting 14 countries. That experience filled my heart with joy and fulfillment, even if the journey was something my mother/hero disapproved of. Funny enough, one day, I also bought a gorgeous house in a neighborhood that was once a dream on a vision board. But I bought it because I wanted it, not for my momma's approval, but for my children and their future.

To women with big, bold dreams that others won't understand, I want to encourage you to see it through for you! Don't regret the life you didn't live, worried about how others view you. Get and stay big for you!

THE PATH FORWARD

We often unconsciously drive ourselves to acquire perfection to gain approval. However, I want to challenge women to gain self-acceptance first to achieve self-actualization and fulfillment! Latinas deserve to shine from within by taking up space in highly successful arenas. We deserve to get & stay big. The key to life is sustaining this elevated state of being to achieve prosperity.

Through my journey, I want to encourage all women - Latinas especially - to ask for help as they level up!

My journey vacillated between pursuing success on my terms and avoiding much-needed help. I've embraced high standards my entire life and bucked many trends by doing what I want, not what society or my family want for me. As such, I often feel judged and misunderstood as I chase after my deepest desires. As I was chasing after my dreams, which came with their fair share of challenges, I often faced challenges alone out of fear of judgment.

I am happy with my growth, success, and self-actualization today. I hope my story will inspire other women to fall in love with their growth, embracing the idea that seeking help is the cheat code for success and that external criticism doesn't matter.

Latinas need each other. If you feel alone, reach out for help from a therapist, life and business coaches, or support groups online. As Latinas, our most significant strength is our legacy of community, and we all deserve it.

ABOUT IRENE

Irene Quevedo is the CEO and Founder of Wealthy Latinas a company with a mission to free the ambition of all women of color. She is co-founder and partner at Level Up Latina where she co-hosts & produces The Level Up Latina Podcast. She is an established C-suite executive with 20+ years of experience in leadership & professional development. Coaching clients work with her to make their biggest dreams a reality.

Irene is a successful author, public speaker, nonprofit leader, and executive coach. For fun she travels (a lot) and is a very proud momma of three teens! Irene's life is one of adventure, a little trial & error, and lots of love.

She serves proudly as the Chief Executive Officer of Operation Jump Start (OJS) Where she began her extensive career in 2009. Prior to this, Irene received a dual Bachelor of Arts degree in Sociology and International Studies from the University of California, Santa Barbara. She also holds an MBA from Eastern University. She backpacked through all of Central America and parts of South America post-college graduation and recently in 2017 with her young family!

As a Latina born and raised in an underserved community, she is indelibly passionate about the work done at Operation Jump Start a youth serving organization that supports underrepresented students to and through college. She is the mission of this work beginning with her life as a first-gen Latina.

With almost two decades of experience in the non-profit sector focused on serving families and children, her passion for the students OJS serves and the organization's mission is second to none. She works closely with the agency's Board of Directors to oversee all office operations including human resources management, technology, marketing, enrichment and academic programming, fundraising efforts as well as financial management systems.

Irene enjoys podcasting and is proud of her consistent work establishing and producing the Level Up Latina podcast.

Learn more and connect with Irene at:

https://www.linkedin.com/in/irene-quevedo
www.wealthylatinas.com

The Level Up Latina Podcast
@wealthy.latinas
@leveluplatina
@queventure.abroad

JENNIFER FRANCO

"Adelante, con ganas que el tiempo es oro"

- Jennifer Franco

~ ~ ~

Jennifer Franco is a first-generation Latina from Chicago who triumphed over adversity to become a beacon of hope in her community. Jennifer is the Founder & President of the Fempreneur Poder Hub, a non-profit that helps inspire women of color to become entrepreneurs. She is a passionate, entrepreneurial leader, who symbolizes empowerment, equity, and transformation.

~ ~ ~

In memoriam of my aunt Maria E. Chacón and dedicated to my loving husband, children, mother, uncle, and all the individuals who have empowered, inspired, or lifted me when I needed it the most. Gracias!

PAVING PATHWAYS TO EMPOWERMENT

THE JOURNEY

My path to becoming the empowering changemaker I am today has been paved with resilience and a deep-rooted commitment to breaking the mold society often tries to cast for women of color, especially Latinas. The most pivotal moments in my journey are framed by a combination of both struggle and breakthroughs, each playing a crucial role in shaping my resolve and direction.

One such turning point came as I was on the cusp of completing my doctoral courses, ready to embark on my dissertation. It was a time filled with both excitement for the future and the harsh reality of the present, as my pursuit of gainful employment was met with offers that neither matched my qualifications nor recognized my potential. The positions available were often underpaid, or I was passed over for leadership roles for which I was not only qualified but also deeply passionate about. It was one devastating blow after another.

While that period of my life was challenging, it was also transformative. It was then that the seeds for the Fempreneur Poder Hub were sown – an organization that I helped found. Our mission is to dismantle obstacles, transcend boundaries, and inspire women of color to bring their fempreneurial visions to life by providing educational resources, tools, and networking opportunities.

The disappointments I faced in the job market fueled a burning desire to create a space where the obstacles I encountered could be dismantled, not just for myself, but for all women of color with entrepreneurial dreams. I wanted to turn my adversities into avenues for others, ensuring a smoother path for those who followed.

My experiences, both positive and negative, have been instrumental in forging my character and ambitions. The positive ones have shown me what is possible, providing glimpses of what can be achieved with dedication and support. The negative experiences, on the other hand, have offered invaluable lessons in tenacity and the importance of self-belief, teaching me that the most profound growth often comes from the most challenging times.

My background and upbringing have been the bedrock of my journey. As a first-generation, low-income, young Latina mother/woman, I've experienced firsthand the complex layers of adversity that come with navigating spaces that were not designed with people like me in mind. My upbringing instilled in me the values of hard work and the importance of community. Still, it highlighted the disparities and barriers that are too common for underrepresented communities. These experiences have not only influenced my path but also the mission of my organization.

My family immigrated from Guatemala, and I am proud of my Mayan roots, where you find la tierra del cafe. My aunt helped my mother come to the States. My aunt was an entrepreneur in Guatemala. She was a street vendor selling pan con frijol and other snacks. She was the first person in my life to discuss being an independent entrepreneur and how discipline required patience. My aunt was always quick on her feet and was an exceptional negotiator. I remember when we went to Logan Square in the old Discount Mega Mall, and she issued a counter offer for a pair of shoes. When we went to local markets, most of the time, she would also try this technique. Sometimes, she was successful, and sometimes not, and I admired her persistence and resilience. When I turned ten years old, she encouraged me to do the same. This was an essential skill that I learned at an early age that now comes in handy when creating partnerships and MOUs (a type of legal report).

I grew up in Albany Park, a neighborhood in the City of Chicago. Back in the mid 1990s most of our community was low-income, and there were no brand store names besides Walgreens and Jewel Osco. During that time, I observed local mom-and-pop stores donde we could ask for fiado and then go back the following day or two and pay our debt.

Living in a diverse community like Albany Park was great, especially because most of the businesses were owned by Latinos during that time. Now, as I am older and reflecting on this aspect, I see that it demonstrates the power of the Latino community and entrepreneurial spirit.

My uncle is another person who has served as a significant wellspring of inspiration and influence in my life. He, too, has been a lifelong entrepreneur, having run his own DJ business for two decades and now partnering with his wife to run a successful cleaning business. He encouraged me to take a leap of faith and open my own nonprofit business.

I'll never forget the words he said the day I asked his advice about starting my own nonprofit: "ve y mira que pasa lo peor que puede pasar es que nadie llegue al evento inaugural y fracases. Si no arriesgas nunca vas a saber."

As I write this, I have concluded my doctoral courses. It's important for me to share that there have been many struggles along the way. One such struggle is attending a predominantly white institution. Although the program strives to assist its students of color who are first-generation, there are some important considerations that often get overlooked. For example, many of us who are pursuing doctoral degrees and are interested in becoming entrepreneurs do not have the same access to tools or resources as some of our peers. This limits our opportunities to find our footing or form those pivotal connections that can propel our careers and professional endeavors. I've also realized that the significance of the hidden curriculum in education is paramount, and its teaching should not be considered less important than the specific content of a course or technical skills. The skills and understanding derived from the hidden curriculum are crucial for success in life, extending well beyond the confines of the classroom or specific professional fields.

For example, students who have the time and availability to work as graduate assistants or researchers have a pathway and direct connection to people working or teaching in their chosen field. They can ask for guidance, advice, or help to navigate their career choices. However, people like me, with limited resources and connections within the research field, find it challenging to balance all of our commitments excluding us from opportunities like fellowships, graduate assistantships, and more. My job and my duties as a mother and board member keep me busy and limit my availability to take on additional commitments.

Recently, as I contemplated my career path, reality struck me—I was nearing the end of my doctoral courses with no job offer in hand. Five months of relentless applications to over 50 corporations, institutions, and organizations yielded responses expressing admiration for my credentials but ultimately favoring other candidates. I'd undergone first, second, and even third rounds of interviews, delving into the hiring process only to face rejection. The experience even led me to scrutinize my physical and verbal cues, questioning whether to disclose my doctoral journey or not. What was I missing?

I'd been having discussions that highlighted the gaps in my doctoral program and forced me to confront the reality of the student loans I'd amassed in pursuing my doctoral degree. Many people I spoke with agreed that we'd chosen to pursue higher education with the promises of an expansive job market and financial success. However, despite tapping into our individual networks and jumping through all the recommended hoops, the barriers to employment were still too high. The current economic climate, marked by wars and high inflation, has made securing employment daunting. Job applications flood in by the dozen, with recruiters sifting through hundreds of candidates in mere hours.

How could I stand out? Moreover, how could I empower other women facing similar challenges to stand out as well? We may lack the right connections but have grit, drive, talent, and wisdom. I yearned for establishing a space where we could unite, collaboratively elevating and connecting one another.

Those conversations proved invaluable as they led me to a staggering insight and an inspired idea. The answer was right in front of me – I didn't have to wait for the suitable spaces to appear or the right opportunities to come along – I could CREATE THEM! I decided right then to take a leap of faith. I wanted to create a place for people like me to talk about the student loans we'd racked up, our frustrations in the job market, and how to navigate a path forward together.

I also knew that many women, specifically Black and Latina women, were struggling to find jobs that would provide the flexibility to work from home or offer other incentives that would help offset some other aspects of their personal lives, for example, allowing mothers to leave at a particular time to pick up their children, offering DCAP, or creating hybrid options that would be flexible to working mothers/caretakers.

From this, The Fempreneur Poder Hub was born. It embodies my journey—a testament to a path shaped by both the shadows of bias and the light of perseverance. The challenges I faced are not unique; indeed, they reflect a broader systemic issue. According to the 2022 Stanford Latino Entrepreneurship Initiative report, Latino businesses face challenges in accessing financing, receiving smaller and fewer contracts from corporations and governments, and encountering longer approval times for loans and contracts. This reality underscores the critical need for the services we provide at the Fempreneur Poder Hub. It's a hub designed to provide what I once longed for and believe is essential for progress: education, resources, tools, and a support network to empower women of color to turn their entrepreneurial visions into reality. This nonprofit isn't just a response to the barriers I've faced; it's la esperanza for change and a platform for empowerment, reflecting my life's work as a changemaker dedicated to uplifting others.

THE LEARNINGS

The journey I've embarked upon has been punctuated with profound struggles and unexpected turns. Each challenge faced has been a building block, shaping the foundations of my resilience and purpose.

One of the most pivotal challenges I encountered was becoming a young mother while still in high school. The difficulty of this experience was multifaceted as I navigated the complexities of early motherhood alongside the pressures and expectations of academic life. The sense of isolation was palpable; the school environment, peers, and even administrators often cast a shadow of ostracization and shame rather than offering support.

When I became pregnant, I recall a particular conversation that I had with a school administrator who strongly encouraged me to move to an alternative all-girl school focused on pregnant teenagers. It was implied that the school felt that I would be a distraction and a bad example for my classmates. I had multiple bad experiences in high school that could've discouraged me or thrown me off track, but I held my resolve and pushed forward.

You never really know the impact you can make on a young person, and I often think of my special education math teacher and if she knows how much her support and encouragement changed my entire life. Her guidance motivated me to pursue higher education, a prospect that had never crossed my mind.

Navigating early motherhood presented many unique challenges. No one prepared me for how often young babies had to go to the pediatrician's office for regular checkups. Being young and having a mother who couldn't drive or speak English, requesting early dismissal was intimidating for her, so I took it upon myself to skip certain class periods, ensuring I could get home in time for the baby's appointments. To not miss any assignments, I often enlisted the help of other students to share their notes and catch me up on what I'd missed so I could maintain my GPA. Looking back, I am still in awe of how I managed it all.

The emotional burden was compounded by motherhood's physical and mental demands and the pursuit of my education. In facing these challenges, my inner strength was forged through a combination of tenacity and courage. I drew upon a deep-seated resolve, an understanding that my actions were not just for my immediate benefit, but also as a tribute to the sacrifices made by my mother and aunt. Their journey to provide a better life for our family in a new country served as my guiding light and greatest motivation. It was never about obligation; it was about honoring sus sacrificios with my achievements.

I came up with strategies that proved effective in overcoming these trials that were rooted in a mindset that viewed obstacles as opportunities to prove my capabilities. I focused on setting small, achievable goals, celebrating each accomplishment as a step towards a larger vision. I embraced my education not just as a route to personal advancement but as a tool for changing the narrative for myself and my family.

People often ask how I persevered through those challenges, and I think it's important to share that what kept me going was a deep sense of wanting to succeed and feeling supported by everyone who came before me.

My support system was not formed from those physically present; rather, the intangible presence of my loved ones' hopes and sueños held me steadfast. Without an immediate support network, I turned to los dichos y cuentos de la familia, their aspirations, and their belief in the promise of a better future as my guide.

A perfect example of this is my aunt, who, while on her own entrepreneurship journey, didn't live close by and passed away when I was an adult, but her memory and her stories kept me going. I'd think of how much I wanted to be like her – someone who dedicated her life to caring for others. She believed in me and provided words of wisdom and love exactly when I needed them, even when I didn't ask. She intervened on my behalf with my mother when I found out I was pregnant. My Mom had been really unhappy with my teen pregnancy, and it led to a lot of tension, but my Aunt knew how much I'd need support and helped mend my relationship with my mother and help us communicate. Even as I write this, I can feel how proud she'd be of how far I have come and all the beautiful things I'm building for women like her.

Challenging established norms and disrupting the status quo became a hallmark of my experience. In becoming a young mother in high school, I defied the expectations of those who saw only a statistic rather than a determined individual. My continued pursuit of education was a statement against a narrative that often writes off young mothers as lost causes. This defiance extended beyond personal boundaries as I began to confront and combat the systemic barriers I and many others faced.

It led to the creation of the Fempreneur Poder Hub, a sanctuary for other women of color to find education, resources, and support, countering the narrative that had once threatened to define me. The most significant learning from my journey is that resilience is not a trait you are born with but one that is built through enduring and overcoming adversity. It is understanding that the collective hopes of those who came before you can be the wind beneath your wings, propelling you forward when the path is murky. It is realizing that one's worth is not determined by how society labels you but by the courage you show in the face of those labels and the tenacity with which you carve your own path. This understanding is what has shaped me into the person I am today.

THE INSPIRATION

Throughout my life, inspiration, and motivation have come from various sources, each carrying me through the ebb and flow of my journey's challenges. In my earlier years, especially when I faced the daunting reality of being a young mother in high school, my foremost inspirations were my mother and aunt. Their decision to leave their home country and come to the United States bore the promise of new beginnings for them and future generations. The sheer scale of their sacrifice, the weight of their dreams, and their unyielding esperanza inspired me to persevere. They embodied a silent strength I sought to emulate, a resilience that whispered of potential and opportunity amidst the toughest times.

During the times when I felt ostracized at school or undervalued in the job market, it wasn't just the people in my life that provided inspiration, but also the stories and struggles of historical figures and the potent words found within the pages of books. I found solace and strength in the narratives of others like Gloria Anzaldúa, Sandra Cisneros, and Audre Lorde who had faced adversity and triumphed. Stories of powerful women who had changed the course of history, and who had stood firm in the face of societal and systemic challenges, became a beacon for me. They were reminders that my path, while fraught with its own unique challenges, was part of a larger tapestry of shared struggle and collective triumph.

As my journey unfolded and my aspirations evolved, so did my sources of inspiration. The moment I decided to establish the Fempreneur Poder Hub, my motivation was fueled not only by my past experiences but also by the potential impact on others' lives. I became inspired by the community I sought to serve—the aspiring women entrepreneurs whose vibrant dreams were often dimmed by the barriers they faced.

The vision of creating a space where these women could flourish, empowered by education and support, was driven by a desire to transform adversity into opportunity, not just for myself but for the countless others who shared my story in one form or another.

Over time, my inspiration became less about individual survival and more about collective upliftment. It transformed from a personal quest into a communal mission, reflecting a shift from overcoming my own struggles to dismantling the barriers for others. This evolution of inspiration rooted in personal history but branching out into collective empowerment has been the cornerstone of my motivation, propelling me forward and fueling my commitment to advocacy, leadership, and change.

THE ADVICE

My advice to my younger self would be to embrace patience and trust in your unique timing. Success doesn't adhere to a universal schedule, and when your moment to shine arrives, it will be undeniably yours, tailored to the narrative of your struggles and triumphs.

Even if it feels like your efforts are unseen, remember that someone is always watching, and the impact of your work extends far beyond immediate recognition.

Lean into the rich tapestry of your Latinidad! For me, it was recognizing the beauty of my skin color and my Mayan ancestry as a source of strength, not a barrier. Your authentic self is your greatest asset; it's what sets you apart and what will draw others to your cause and vision. Hold onto that authenticity as you navigate the challenges ahead.

To those walking a similar path, remember that resilience is often silent, but never unnoticed. The habits of perseverance, setting small but intentional goals, and nurturing a network, even if it's initially invisible, are essential. To build your network attend networking events, join professional associations, become part of an associate board for a nonprofit, and engage with online communities related to your industry. Building a strong network can open doors to new opportunities, partnerships, and support systems. Go beyond mere networking by cultivating an inner circle of individuals who will strengthen your sense of comunidad. Your journey is your own, but it's woven into a larger collective struggle where every step forward can be a beacon for others. Embrace your story, pace, and heritage as each is a powerful ingredient in the alchemy of your success.

THE PATH FORWARD

To my fellow Latinas who share the path of dreams and determination, I stand with you, my story interlaced with yours in a mosaic of struggle, resilience, and triumph. The legacy I hope to inspire is one of empowerment where each of us harnesses our collective challenges as fuel to ignite change and build bridges to futures bright with promise. Let my journey be a testament that your origins, while they shape you, do not confine you. Your voice is powerful, your experiences are valid, and your potential is limitless.

I urge you to step forward with the courage of your convictions, to embrace the unique strength that lies in our shared heritage, and to lean into the beauty of your Latinidad. It is not just a part of who you are es el super poder que mueve montañas. My call to action is this: Walk boldly in the direction of your sueños, arm in arm with your hermanas y comunidad who share your journey.

Establish spaces where our stories are not just told, but heard and where our dreams are not deferred, but realized. Support one another, lift each other up, and never underestimate the transformative power of a united community. Let us be the architects of a future where a Latina's place is anywhere she chooses it to be—where our daughters will inherit a world not of barriers, but of boundless opportunity. Together, let's build that world. Adelante, con ganas que el tiempo es oro.

POEMA: BORDERLAND IDENTITIES

¿Quien sera esa mujer en el espejo?
¿Sera Latina o Americana?
¿Hablará español o Inglés?
¿Vendrá de riquezas o pobreza?
¿Tendrá educación superior?
¿Será estudiante de posgrado?
¿Ha de ser estudiosa, notable y exitosa?

Maybe she is all that and more
Talvez nadie sepa de todos sus logros y fracasos
Quizas se esconde detras de una fachada to protect herself from those that
envy her
Talvez se protege de aquellos who once made her feel inferior y la
desprecian por su color de piel

NOW, ella es segura de si misma
Ahora ella es una lider exitosa
Ahora ella acepta sus complexities
NOW, she has found out who that woman is
Una mezcla Latinoamericana, bilingüe en dos idiomas
Y no se preocupa del que dirán

Ella es Jennifer Franco, mamá, educadora, e hija de
Maria que proviene de la ciudad de Guatemala.

ABOUT JENNIFER

Jennifer, a first-generation, Latina from Chicago, triumphed over adversity to become a beacon of hope in her community. Overcoming challenges from an unsupportive educational environment and the hardships of a single-mother household, she was inspired by key mentors who helped her propel in her professional and educational career. Jennifer transformed from doubting her college prospects to holding an M.A. in Women & Gender Studies from Loyola and a B.A. in Political Science from NEIU. Currently pursuing a PhD in Higher Education at Loyola University Chicago, she is recognized for her dedication to eradicating racial and ethnic achievement disparities. With over five years in academia, Jennifer's roles in various institutions emphasize her passion for mentorship and community upliftment. Jennifer's bilingual skills enhance her ability to connect with and empower diverse communities. Nominated for the United Latinas Extraordinary Latinas Awards 2023 and the ATHENA Women of Influence Award in 2022, her achievements mirror her dedication. As a teenage mom, her resilience further exemplifies her commitment to redefining narratives for underserved communities. Jennifer is now the Founder and President of the Fempreneur Poder Hub a non-profit that helps inspire women of color to become entrepreneurs. A passionate entrepreneurial leader, she symbolizes empowerment, equity, and transformation.

Learn more about how you can contribute to a future where every woman has the opportunity to thrive as an entrepreneur. Together, let's build a world of limitless possibilities. Connect with Jennifer at:

www.linkedin.com/in/jennifer-c-franco
https://www.linkedin.com/company/fempreneur-poder-hub/
https://fempreneurpoder.com/
Instagram: @fempreneurpoderhub

SCAN ME

JENNIFER GUZMAN

"By recognizing the divine power within each of us, women can navigate the intersection of roles of both motherhood and entrepreneurship with authenticity, & confidence."

- Jennifer Guzman

~ ~ ~

Jennifer ("Jen") is a multifaceted professional, assuming roles as a mompreneur, educator, leader, and consultant, all anchored by her diverse background in Science, Finance, and Administration. Jen is the founder and CEO of Bright Tax Corp and a chapter leader for Women Warriors Latina Collab in the New York City area.

~ ~ ~

Above all, I am grateful to God for allowing me to share pivotal chapters of my life, empowering women around the world.

To my mother, Teresa, a beacon of selflessness. Your unwavering dedication, and your superhero-like strength inspire me daily. As I navigate motherhood myself, I discover a deeper love, respect, and admiration for you. I wish the world had more souls as special as yours.

Finally, to my son, who has transformed my life in ways I could never have anticipated. Every day, you unveil new lessons about motherhood and reveal facets of myself. Your presence uplifts me, bringing smiles even on the cloudiest days. You are my divine gift, and I've pledged to protect you forever.

You are and will forever be the light of my life!

REDISCOVERING OUR TRUE SELVES AND EMBRACING EMPOWERMENT

THE JOURNEY

My family and ancestors are from the Dominican Republic, an island surrounded by a vast blue sea of beautiful crystal clear water, tropical weather that caresses your skin, adorned with lush green mountains, fresh air, and people who show you the true meaning of generosity.

It was here where I was born, where I learned the value of hard work, how to value and respect others, and always help and serve regardless of who they are. During my first 8 years, I learned the value of family, saw the value of sacrifice, and became acutely aware of the pernicious impact of poverty and the absence of education.

My grandparents, deprived of formal schooling, not by choice, worked the land from a very early age. It was the only means to survive and provide. Despite migrating to urban areas in search of familial stability and opportunities, they were confined to only average jobs. Yet, in their circumstances, they found the determination to thrive and establish a "normal life". Their resilience, born out of historical struggles, has been a guiding force in my journey as a single mother, a professional, and an entrepreneur.

For as long as I can recall, my grandfather possessed an entrepreneurial spirit within him. He created items from wood to resell, alongside managing the only barbershop in his small town. His skills extended to crafting drums and guitars from scratch. Additionally, he harbored a profound and obsessive passion for medicine. He taught himself how to read in order to educate himself and explore holistic ways to heal people. My mother inherited her creativity and tenacity from him, and while they didn't lack vision, their financial limitations hindered their ability to pursue their passions.

Conversely, my grandmother epitomized the role of a devoted wife and mother within the limitations of societal expectations. The women in our community are not expected to be providers or be financially independent. For generations, many of the women in my family were only taught to be devoted housewives with no voice and no education. So, it is easy to understand that their options were limited.

In contrast, my parents endeavored to break free from these lineal norms. My mother, in particular, continually emphasized the virtues of obtaining a good education, learning our values as women (not as a wife), and having our finances in order. She always said, "I only want you to do better than grandma and me. I just want the best for you. I do not want you to experience the same struggles we have encountered". She also imparted upon me the belief that the pursuit of knowledge should be cherished, for its value transcends mere academic accolades.

As an immigrant, my struggles extended beyond assimilation into a new culture, lifestyle, and other things; I struggled the most with identity. It was incredibly challenging to fit into a society where our values didn't align, language barriers and physical appearance labeled me as the "weird one" or the "outsider", my accent was a source of shame, and my sense of fashion was outdated. As an 8-year-old who left everything behind to pursue the so-called "American Dream," it was disheartening to face the reality of not belonging.

While I drew inspiration in various aspects of my upbringing, both in schools, and within my family, there were many things I desired to change as I felt it was my duty to do so. However, I felt daunted by the enormity of the task ahead.

Motivated by the adversities endured by my parents and grandparents, I forced myself to get through school, earning a Bachelor's in Science and nearing completion of a Ph.D. (having early on settled for a Master's). This endeavor was driven not by personal ambition but by a desire to honor my family; As I was not doing it for me, but for them. My accomplishments always felt more theirs than mine; hence I never found a valid reason to celebrate them. I continued pursuing these academic achievements as it was my duty to do it to make my family proud (and just like that, I became a people pleaser). This resulted in a profound disconnect between my own aspirations for fulfillment and joy and my familial expectations.

As a people pleaser, my feelings of not being fulfilled professionally didn't matter; I was more scared to disappoint them. For the first time in six years, I realized that I had drowned in professional dissatisfaction, losing touch with my true essence and my true self in the process (I no longer knew what brought me joy). This internal conflict made me realize that my definition of success differed greatly from theirs. Their version meant having a six-figure job, climbing the corporate ladder, and retiring with an impressive pension plan.

After initiating a journey of self-discovery, early on in 2022, I understood the true measure of success in my life. True success, for me, entailed aligning my pursuits with personal passion and purpose and I realized I was not going to achieve it in a corporate job setting.

Thus, I ventured onto the path of entrepreneurship, driven by a fervent desire to cause tangible change within my community and motivated to specifically serve Latina women who have faced adversity and challenges similar to those I have experienced in my own life. Women, just like me, who feel unheard, undervalued, overlooked, and looking for support systems that understand their cultural context and challenges. Armed with the knowledge gleaned from my own experiences in an industry dominated by men, I seek to support, empower, & provide resources to improve their financial literacy, overcome obstacles, and facilitate their socio-economic advancement.

Becoming the empowering changemaker I am today is a journey that has been shaped by transformative moments and intense experiences, particularly around motherhood, postpartum depression, and embracing single motherhood while navigating my quest for fulfillment and happiness. Perhaps the most significant battle waged war against the expectations surrounding roles as a mother, provider, and professional.

Motherhood was a significant turning point in my life. A woman's power is her innate ability to create and nurture. I don't think I ever understood that until I had a little seed growing in my womb. It took me by surprise. Honestly, I wasn't ready for motherhood, but then again, I'm not sure if I was ever supposed to feel prepared for it.

For a second, the thought of motherhood seemed like the worst thing because of how everyone would perceive me "as a disappointment." Within the traditional framework of my family nucleus, academic achievements and professional success held precedence over familial pursuits. For many years, my worth was attached to all my academic achievements, and my time was only invested in those pursuits.

Yet, when I found out I was carrying a beautiful gift inside my womb, being seen as disappointment didn't matter anymore. What scared me the most was the fear of not being able to love this tiny human growing inside of me. I didn't love myself. I didn't date for love. Who was I to give love when love wasn't given to me?

Love is such a vague and foreign sentiment, frequently disguised as lust. At 22 years old, I still saw myself as a girl, not a woman. However, this juncture marked the initiation of a personal journey, a journey towards self-discovery and purpose. This was part of my journey to grow into the woman God has created me to be. If I didn't know what love was and I didn't know how to love, then becoming a young mother was my opportunity to start learning.

On December 12th, 2020, at 1:18 AM, my firstborn changed my given name to Mommy. When I first saw him, I couldn't take my eyes off his rosy bunny cheeks and his glazed brown eyes. At that moment, I just knew I was meant to find him in my existence. While I held him for the first time in those fleeting moments, he became the missing piece, the embodiment of a love that transcended the tangible. I understood that the most profound experiences elude description—they are felt.

Overwhelmed by fears, I embarked on this new chapter of my life as a mother, unprepared yet ready to conquer all that must be conquered.

One thing I was not ready to battle in my journey of motherhood was postpartum depression. Yet, I felt forced to wrestle with this monster in silence, thus compounding the challenges of single motherhood.

My son is now 3 years old, and only a year ago, I chose to break the silence surrounding my battle with postpartum depression and domestic violence. Why keep silent, some might ask? The sad truth is most women do, but my decision to remain silent stemmed from cultural norms—topics like these were taboo within the confines of my traditional upbringing. Things like this were certainly never discussed at the dinner table. On the other hand, I was familiar with small-town gossip about struggling new moms who were quickly labeled "crazy" and incapable of being a mother.

The fear of being labeled as "crazy" and "incapable" perpetuates the silence that many women endure. I didn't want my own family to judge me for what I was going through.

When I finally decided to share on social media about my experience, my grandfather, who I deeply adore, called me to echo his traditional beliefs, dismissing my struggles as evil feelings and attributing them to a lack of prayer. His words stung like fire. I was so disappointed. I didn't dare to defend myself and own my truth. So I sat quietly, zoning out until his words sounded like mumbling, when suddenly, the silence in my head ignited a realization—I could not allow others to negate my truth.

The power of owning and standing for my truth became evident. Despite familial skepticism, my experience was mine to navigate, survive, and overcome, not because it was luck but because God's purpose was to use my story as a testament to his love and grace.

Despite the many hardships I encountered, my family's unconditional love and support became a guiding light, sustaining me through the darkest moments. The birth of my child also marked a profound awakening, but it also ushered in numerous challenges. Balancing newfound roles and responsibilities amidst an identity crisis pushed me to a breaking point, which became my version of hitting rock bottom. At this critical point, I faced a pivotal choice: remain a victim of circumstance or harness the pain into a driving force for positive change.

This redirection marked a monumental shift. Embracing the role of a single mother and unemployed, I returned to my parents' little 2-bedroom apartment in Washington Heights, determined to pursue a Ph.D. as a pathway to a brighter future for my child. This period of upheaval and reinvention led me back to entrepreneurship, infusing it with a renewed perspective and purpose.

My parents played pivotal roles during this season as well. They showed up for me in the most unexpected and unimaginable ways. My mother quit her job to take care of my son full time while I was juggling the responsibilities of academia, single parenthood, and entrepreneurship while my father provided some financial support. It was an intensely challenging time. Doubts loomed, whispering of impending failure within the chaos of managing multiple roles. Yet, this journey unveiled hidden reserves of strength and resilience within me, and most importantly, I grew to love, respect, and admire my parents even more. Contrary to my fears, I found myself not merely surviving but thriving amidst the overwhelming odds stacked against me.

That season of my life showcased the strength born from adversity. It illuminated the transformative power of perseverance, resilience, and the ability to turn pain into purpose. Through it all, I discovered that every trial

I faced, every tear I shed, was not in vain. They served as catalysts for my growth.

Through this life-changing path, I have evolved into an empowering force, driven by the belief that shattered moments can indeed shine brilliantly when touched by the light of determination and resilience.

As a First-Gen Latina business owner who intimately understands the pain points and struggles of growing a business while juggling numerous roles (particularly that of a single mom), I see my story and my business, skills, and knowledge as an opportunity to create a supportive community and platform where other women feel heard, valued, and empowered. Despite facing ongoing obstacles, I'm committed to embracing the path that God uniquely designed for me, constructing a life that allows me to forge unique memories with my son and parents while also aiding other women to do the same for themselves.

For me, success doesn't look like millions of dollars. It looks like living life on my own terms and having the opportunity to leave a mark on the lives of other young women in my community. Most importantly, it means allowing my parents to experience true joy and repaying their sacrifices.

THE LEARNINGS

Navigating the complexities of single motherhood, the fear of being judged, the struggle to comprehend love, and my insecurities about having the ability to successfully run a business on my own, compounded by postpartum depression, fueled a redirection in my life's trajectory.

This new season in my life demanded a profound understanding that prioritizing my peace and happiness surpassed conforming to a dysfunctional familial structure. However, I found myself at a loss for where to start or how to navigate this shift. I know many other women can relate with this struggle. Growing up, I never witnessed my mother or grandmother prioritizing their own emotional and/or physical well-being, despite their exceptional caregiving and nurturing roles. As a result, I didn't have a supportive female figure to confide in or seek guidance.

Throughout the first months of my solitary journey, I turned to various strategies and coping mechanisms to cope with these challenges. Although embracing the power of self-reflection and journaling became a sanctuary to freely express and find solace in untangling complex emotions, I always sensed that something else was missing. Seeking resolution, I started therapy with the goal of finding that inner peace, reconnecting with my true self, releasing the grudges I held, and extending forgiveness to those who had caused me deep emotional and physical pain. Yet, I soon discovered that while these strategies were somewhat efficient, they fell short of my expectations.

The true transformations started to unfold when I began to cultivate a spiritual relationship with God. Turning to God with my struggles, my hurt, my traumas, fears, and worries sparked an indescribable shift within me that I continue to foster to this day.

In confronting these challenges, I discovered the power of resilience, inner fortitude, and the ability to rewrite my narrative. Each hurdle became a stepping stone, propelling me forward and reinforcing the notion that disruption and defiance against norms can lead to personal empowerment and growth.

THE INSPIRATION

Throughout my life, my most profound inspiration stemmed from the women within my family, particularly my mother and grandmother. However, this realization didn't dawn on me until I became a mother myself.

Before motherhood, my inspiration often stemmed from shallow, materialistic pursuits that I associated with success and fulfillment. It wasn't until I embarked on the journey of motherhood that my entire perspective underwent a profound shift, a redefinition for life and who I was meant to be.

Motherhood served as a catalyst, unveiling the immeasurable value embodied by the women in my family. My mother and grandmother, in their own ways, demonstrated aspects I deeply admire and aspire to replicate in my life while revealing traits I aimed to alter.

The two qualities that resonated deeply with me were their unwavering commitment and relentless fortitude. Witnessing their perseverance and determination to uphold marital vows and their core morals and values left an indelible mark on me. These traits are essential, not only in the realm of family life but also as an entrepreneur navigating challenges in the pursuit of success. I've learned that commitment and grit make the difference between achieving greatness and succumbing to adversity.

These women, my family's matriarchs and guiding lights, have crucial roles. They've empowered the men in our family to achieve their goals by standing as pillars of support. They've taught me the importance of asserting myself in relationships, recognizing my worth, and standing firm in my convictions.

Moreover, the experience of unconditional love became vividly evident to me after I became a mother and confronted the challenges of single parenthood. I mean, what type of mother sacrifices a full-time stable job to care for her grandson? What type of parents risk their financial stability to provide support to a grown woman with a newborn? If that isn't unconditional love, then I don't know what is.

Their constant support and love spoke volumes. It altered my brain chemistry. It was a profound testament to the power of unconditional parental love, reassuring me that regardless of my circumstances, their love and support remained strong because I was their daughter.

These experiences and the resilience of the women in my family continue to be my guiding light, shaping my values, aspirations, and determination to navigate life's challenges with unwavering commitment and unconditional love.

THE ADVICE

Reflecting on my journey, there are invaluable lessons I would impart to my younger self and to anyone traversing a similar path.

Firstly, I've learned the significance of not allowing "bad" experiences to define us. Rather than hiding behind the scars and wounds that life has etched upon us, embracing and honoring them is pivotal. These experiences, however painful, have forged the strength and resilience we yearn for, imparting invaluable wisdom along the way.

The process of revisiting these old scars, acknowledging their impact on my journey, serve as reminders of my starting points, the mistakes, and the lessons that were worth learning. A celebration of my personal evolution.

In my journey, I recognized the importance of releasing pent-up feelings and thoughts. Bottling emotions proved detrimental, prompting me to adopt the habit of journaling. Writing became a sanctuary where I could express myself freely, finding solace in being heard—speaking not just to myself but also to a higher power. Through this practice, I discovered more about myself and found peace with both past and present. Additionally, seeking therapy was the best decision I had ever made.

One profound lesson that reverberates is the understanding that events from the past cannot be altered. Accepting this truth has been liberating. We cannot wish, cry, or ignore the past. The true power lies in altering our understanding of those events, shaping our present and future perspectives.

Amidst the demands of motherhood and entrepreneurship, it was easy to view and to perceive these pursuits as solitary endeavors. Do you feel alone in your journey? I often felt alone. It wasn't until I discovered the immense value in seeking out and belonging to a community of diverse women, fostering mutual growth and support. Connecting with like-minded women with similar aspirations, and also understood my struggles and pains proved invaluable in navigating my own challenges and embracing growth opportunities.

In summary, my advice to my younger self and those on a similar journey is to embrace life's scars as catalysts for growth, release pent-up emotions through journaling, seek a supportive community, understand the importance of commitment, and acknowledge the unchangeable past while reshaping our understanding of it. These pivotal shifts in mindset and practices have significantly contributed to my personal evolution and empowerment.

THE PATH FORWARD

Through sharing my story, I aspire to leave a legacy that sparks an awakening in other women, mothers, and mompreneurs—a call to reconnect with their inherent power. My aim is to inspire the recognition and celebration of our divinity and adaptability as women. The many roles we juggle are facets of our lives, but they do not solely define who we are.

Somewhere along our journeys, we often lose sight of our truest selves. Yet, within each of us lies a choice and an inherent capability to unlock our potential and rise above. I believe we can harmonize our various roles and responsibilities to exist within them and thrive and manifest the life we envision.

My message is one of empowerment—an encouragement to recognize the reservoir of strength within and to reclaim our authenticity. I invite others to embrace their multifaceted nature without allowing these roles to overshadow their core essence. It's a call to action, urging women to step into their power.

Ultimately, I hope that through my story, others will find inspiration to honor their true selves, acknowledge their capabilities, allowing them to unleash their potential to navigate life's complexities while pursuing their dreams with purpose.

ABOUT JENNIFER

Jennifer ("Jen") is a multifaceted professional, assuming roles as a mompreneur, educator, leader, and consultant, all anchored by her diverse background in Science, and Finance, and Administration.

Her accomplishments extend to becoming a best-selling author in "Never Fear Your Fire," a collaborative book co-authored by Women Warriors Collab. This inspiring book seeks to uplift and motivate women by sharing real stories of resilience. Beyond her literary accolades, Jen serves as a chapter leader for Women Warriors Latina Collab in the New York City area, catering to the needs of the Spanish-speaking women's community.

In her capacity as the founder and CEO of Bright Tax Corp., Jen has established a highly regarded tax and accounting firm, committed to empowering and uplifting the Latino community, particularly first-generation Latino entrepreneurs. Through financial literacy and tailored financial services, the firm equips them to forge strong financial foundations, fostering the creation of long lasting legacies.

Despite the taboos and stigmas enveloping mental health, Jen fervently shares her journey as a survivor of domestic violence and as a mother triumphing over severe postpartum depression and anxiety.

Jen embraces the role of a mother to a delightful two-year-old. As a single parent, her foremost commitment lies in being an attentive mother and effectively allocating her time to cultivate a strong bond with her son.

Learn more and connect with Jennifer at:

www.linkedin.com/in/ceo-jguzmanp
https://brighttaxsc.net/

LAURA CAMILA RIVERA

"Our greatest strength lies in our ability to lead with community and purpose. By doing so, we don't just reach our own goals, we also pave the way for future generations of Latinas to succeed.

-   Laura Camila Rivera

~ ~ ~

Laura Camila Rivera is a seasoned marketing expert and the Founder and CEO of CAMI Studio, a San Juan-based agency specializing in equity-centered marketing solutions. Her work has not only impacted her immediate community but has also earned her recognition. Laura secured a spot in El Mundo Boston's Latino 30 Under 30 in 2022 as well as the inaugural ALX100 Influential Latinos, and the 2023 40 Under 40 Powerlist by COLOR Magazine, solidifying her as a leader in both the marketing and Latinx communities.

~ ~ ~

THRIVING TOGETHER: INCLUSIVE LEADERSHIP AND COLLECTIVE GROWTH

THE JOURNEY

Growing up in a bicultural environment has deeply shaped my life and character. Alternating between living in Puerto Rico and Florida, I experienced the richness of two distinct cultures. This bicultural upbringing also brought some unique challenges, especially feeling 'othered.' In Florida, I was the Latina, and people were surprised to hear me speak English "well," while back in Puerto Rico, I was the girl from the States. These experiences taught me about the complexities of identity and belonging from a young age.

My childhood was characterized by constant movement; attending 12 different schools was a norm due to my parents' dedication to church planting. This nomadic lifestyle exposed me to various environments and often placed me in schools where my classmates were from more affluent backgrounds. I learned early on how to navigate diverse socio-economic territories and find commonality in varying settings.

For my first job out of college, I was hired as a Marketing Associate at Kotter Inc, a boutique change leadership consulting firm founded by Dr. John Kotter, a pillar in the Harvard business arena. I learned so much, but I also was one of only three Latinos in the entire organization. I went on to work at the Commonwealth Corporation in a position I was able to find because a Latina I met through ALPFA reached out to me about the opportunity at an organization where she was a board member. She recommended me, and I was hired and started as Marketing Manager within the month. After six months, I was promoted to Associate Director of Marketing. A year later, I was promoted to Director of Marketing. At this point, there was no more runway for me to grow without stepping into the C-Suite. That is when I decided to go off on my own!

I established CAMI Studio in 2021, a marketing agency dedicated to supporting BIPOC and Women-Owned small businesses. At CAMI Studio, I combined automation, creative storytelling, and marketing innovation expertise to help clients achieve their goals while fostering growth and success in diverse communities.

Over the years, the church has served as more than a religious setting for me; it is the foundation of my values and character. Witnessing my parents' dedication, where they consistently put others' needs before their own, I learned to do the same. This quality of overinvesting myself in the service of others, while a foundational driver of my success, also emerged as a double-edged sword. While it pushed me to achieve and to be a leader in my community, it also meant that I often prioritized others' needs to the point of personal exhaustion.

In my professional life, this tendency to overinvest manifested in my roles, where I often found myself as the sole Latina in the room. From Marketing Associate at a change leadership consulting firm, running a DEI Council, to Director of Marketing at a state agency quasi-non-profit, I've always felt a deep sense of responsibility to represent and advocate for my community. This drive led to significant achievements and recognition, but it also meant I was continuously pouring out more than I sometimes had to give. The pressure of being the voice for others, while an honor, was also a heavyweight. Today, I strive for balance in these areas. While it's important for me to serve and elevate others, I've learned that I can do that best by creating space in my life for self-care.

Reflecting on my journey, it's clear that my bicultural background and the lessons learned from a life of constant movement and service have been crucial in shaping who I am. My journey has taught me resilience, the value of representation, and the importance of balancing personal needs with community service. These experiences have molded me into a leader who values community upliftment as much as personal growth and self-care.

THE LEARNINGS

When Hurricane Maria devastated Puerto Rico, I was far from my homeland, and that experience brought a profound sense of helplessness. The most harrowing part was not hearing from my grandmother for days, an unbearable uncertainty. The silence was deafening in those moments, and the worry was all-consuming.

Community has always been my anchor. In response to the crisis, I poured my energy into organizing relief efforts. It wasn't just about helping from a distance; it was about feeling connected to my roots and people. This work was not just necessary but my lifeline, keeping me grounded when everything else seemed to be falling apart.

But this period of intense stress took its toll on me. Throughout my life, I have struggled with an eating disorder and depression, battles that were made tougher by the stigma surrounding mental health in our culture. We often face a wall of silence on these issues in the Latinx community. It's like an unspoken rule that we don't talk about our mental struggles. This cultural barrier made my journey to healing more challenging, but it also ignited in me a purpose – to be open about my struggles.

By sharing my experiences with mental health, I wanted to break this cycle of silence. It's important to me that people in our community know they're not alone. The stigma can be overwhelming, but by speaking out, I hope to chip away at it, to show that it's okay to seek help, to talk about what we're going through.

My turn to community work was more than just a response to a crisis. It was a way to find balance and reconnect with the values central to our culture – solidarity, empathy, and resilience. In working for and with my community,

I found a sense of peace and a way to process my own issues. Ultimately, what brought me back to center was being in Puerto Rico.

What I've come to learn is that everyone is struggling somehow. You can be the happiest, loudest person in a room (which I often was) and still be fighting off demons. In my struggles, I always felt like if I let people know the truth of what I was dealing with, I would be seen as weak, and I would lose people's trust as a leader. It took a lot of courage for me to speak my truth, and when I did, I was amazed by the results.

What I found was that, at the end of the day, my experiences serve as a superpower. People feel comfortable approaching me and being honest. They know one of my leadership values is that I want people to feel empowered to be human, which helps me plan accordingly and support them. They feel safe coming to me with their struggles and challenges and know that I am on their team and cheering them on.

When I was 20, I got a semi-colon tattoo on my wrist. This symbol is well-recognized amongst the mental health community as a symbol for pausing, taking a breath, and continuing forward. By making this my most visible tattoo, I hope to invite people to talk more about it with me. People who aren't familiar with it will ask, and I will tell them about my struggles. People who do know will know they can confide in me. Therein lies the secret to overcoming the fear of talking about our struggles: practice makes perfect.

THE INSPIRATION

In my journey, the fuel that's kept me going, the spark that lit my way, has been a mix of deep-rooted heritage, personal values, and an unwavering commitment to community.

Growing up, I didn't just inherit my Puerto Rican culture; I inherited a legacy of resilience and community spirit. My parents, devoted to their faith and community, were my first real glimpse into what true leadership looks like. It wasn't about titles or accolades but about making a difference and putting others before yourself. That stuck with me, becoming the guiding principle of my life.

Professionally, I've carried this principle with me in every role I've taken on. It was never just about climbing the career ladder but about how I could use my position to help others rise too. Seeing someone's business flourish or a community project come to life because of something I contributed – that's the kind of stuff that keeps me fired up. I've also been incredibly fortunate to cross paths with mentors and sponsors who've been nothing short of transformative in my growth.

With their wisdom and experience, these mentors have shown me different perspectives, challenged me to think bigger, and provided invaluable guidance. For instance, a mentor once introduced me to the 'wheel of life' concept. It's a tool that helps balance different aspects of your life, like career, personal growth, and relationships. I use this tool multiple times a year to keep myself grounded and focused. It's just one example, but it speaks volumes about how mentorship has shaped me.

Each mentor I've encountered has left a unique mark on my path. They've shown me the importance of taking calculated risks, stepping out of my comfort zone, and always keeping the bigger picture in mind. Their belief in me often fueled my confidence to take on new challenges, like spearheading community initiatives or launching my own business.

This mentorship journey hasn't just been about receiving guidance; it's been a two-way street. As much as I've learned from my mentors, I also strive to pay it forward. Whether it's through volunteering, guiding young professionals in their careers, or supporting small business owners, I've aimed to be the kind of leader who empowers others, just as I was empowered.

When Hurricane Maria struck, it was a wake-up call. Despite feeling the crushing helplessness of being away from home, I channeled that energy into organizing relief efforts. It was chaotic and overwhelming, but it taught me the true power of community action.

Starting my own marketing firm wasn't just a career move but a declaration of my commitment to this principle of community upliftment. It's about giving those often overlooked in the business world a fighting chance. Every challenge and success in this venture has reinforced my belief in the power of collective growth.

Looking back at my journey, it's clear that what's driven me is this constant pursuit of meaningful impact. The struggles and the victories have all been part of a larger mission – to uplift, empower, and lead in a way that brings others along.

THE ADVICE

Embrace Your Unique Journey:

I'd say to my younger self and others starting out: Embrace your unique journey, including your cultural heritage and personal experiences. Early on, I struggled with feeling 'othered' due to my bicultural background. However, over time, I realized this unique perspective was a strength, not a liability. It allowed me to connect with diverse groups and understand different viewpoints. Your uniqueness is your superpower – use it to drive change and innovation.

Seek Balance Between Service and Self-Care:

Growing up in a family dedicated to serving others taught me the value of compassion and community. However, it also led to a tendency to overcommit and overlook my needs. I wish I had learned earlier the importance of balancing service with self-care. To those who are natural givers, remember that taking care of yourself isn't selfish; it's necessary. You can't pour from an empty cup. Find practices that replenish you, be it mindfulness, exercise, or pursuing hobbies.

Value Mentorship and Collaboration:

The mentors and sponsors I've had the privilege of learning from have been instrumental in my growth. They've provided guidance, opened doors, and offered perspectives I couldn't see on my own. I would advise anyone, especially those in leadership roles or starting a business, to seek out mentors and be open to collaboration. The wisdom gained from these relationships is invaluable. And remember, mentorship is a two-way street – always look for ways to give back.

It's Okay to Stray from the Path of Perfection:

The pressure to be perfect, especially prevalent in Latino culture, can be stifling. I wish I had realized earlier that it's okay to make mistakes and that perfection isn't the goal – growth is. To anyone struggling under the weight of unrealistic standards, know that it's okay to be imperfect. Learn to view mistakes as opportunities for learning and growth. Set realistic goals, celebrate your progress, and practice self-compassion.

These pieces of advice have been pivotal in my personal and professional development. They've helped shape my approach to leadership, community service, and entrepreneurship, guiding me to where I am today. Remember, your journey is your own – own, learn from, and use it to light the way for others.

THE PATH FORWARD

My understanding of strength has evolved over time, teaching me that its true essence lies in adaptability and inclusivity. This realization dawned early in my journey – strength isn't just about personal resilience or steadfastness; it's fundamentally about embracing change. But not just any change – change that propels not only your growth but also the growth of those around you. This is the core of the leadership philosophy I hold dear – an inclusive leadership that brings everyone along for the ride, making sure no one is left behind.

For me, true leadership transcends the boundaries of personal advancement. It's about creating a space where everyone can thrive together. It's using your influence to pave broader paths, not just for your journey but to make the road more accessible for others to walk with you. It's about recognizing that your growth is intertwined with the growth of your community.

My chapter in this book is my pebble. I'm tossing it out there, hoping it'll resonate with someone. A young Latina may read it and think, "If she could do it, so can I." That's the dream, to light up that spark of change.

So here's my call to action for you: Be bold in your dreams and aspirations, but remember that the real benchmark of your success is measured by how you elevate those around you. Lead in a manner that advances your goals and enriches your community. Because, in the end, the true magic happens when we all grow and succeed together.

ABOUT LAURA

Laura Camila Rivera is a seasoned marketing expert and the Founder and CEO of CAMI Studio, a San Juan-based agency specializing in equity-centered marketing solutions. A graduate of Northeastern University, Laura holds a degree in Business Administration with a concentration in Marketing. Her agency, CAMI Studio, serves a diverse range of clients, including BIPOC organizations and women-owned enterprises, and has been instrumental in fostering community engagement and advocacy. This support has had a transformative impact, setting new benchmarks for how businesses and nonprofits interact with their audiences.

Laura's leadership has been most notable as the Director of Marketing at ALPFA Boston and on the board of Now+There, where she has been a catalyst for positive change and community engagement. She also co-founded the Northeastern Student of Color Caucus (NSCC) and served as the Executive Director of Marketing & Fundraising for the National Puerto Rican Student Caucus, connecting the Puerto Rican Diaspora to meaningful initiatives on the island. Laura's work is particularly impactful in combating the brain drain affecting Puerto Rico, as she is committed to building up the Puerto Rican community both on the island and in the diaspora.

Her work has not only impacted her immediate community but has also earned her recognition. Laura secured a spot in El Mundo Boston's Latino 30 Under 30 in 2022 as well as the inaugural ALX100 Influential Latinos, and the 2023 40 Under 40 Powerlist by COLOR Magazine, solidifying her as a leader in both the marketing and Latinx communities.

Learn more and connect with Laura at:
https://www.cami.studio/
https://www.linkedin.com/in/lauracamilarivera/

LEONELA GONZALEZ-FOGARTY

"Be persistent, determined, and dedicated to pursuing your goal to speak with confidence; don't worry about any mistakes you make. Mistakes are a part of the process of learning a new language."

\- Leonela Gonzalez-Fogarty

~ ~ ~

Leonela Gonzalez-Fogarty is a Venezuelan-American with a Bostonian heart. She is an English Immersion teacher, linguistics, and the CEO of English 4 Life Network, a business that empowers Latino professionals and business owners to connect with the culture and maximize their possibilities by learning English through immersive conversational programs.

~ ~ ~

To my dad, my best role model of entrepreneurship and resilience shining from the sky.
To my mother, siblings, nephews, family and friends for their unconditional love and support in every stage of my life.
To my husband, Kevin Fogarty, for his love and unlimited support including the editing of this chapter , and his five kids and four dogs, my new American family and home.
To all my Latina friends, students, powerhouses mothers, wifes, professionals, and business owners for inspiring me every step of the way.
To all my American friends "Language Panas", mentors, volunteers, teachers and collaborators who have been such an important part of this journey.

EMPOWERING LATINA IMMIGRANT PROFESSIONALS THROUGH LANGUAGE CONFIDENCE

THE JOURNEY

I never thought my education journey would be nearly as long and varied as it has been, and I wouldn't change a thing.

I grew up in Caracas, Venezuela, where you are taught from a young age to find your way and not depend on the government to solve your problems. Due to the lack of good public schools, my parents enrolled me in an excellent private elementary school with an innovative approach: learn by doing. Going to this school taught me to be proactive in solving problems, so even though my English was limited to the small amount taught in school, I applied to a Master's program in the USA. I was sure I would be able to learn what I needed to know.

It was 1996, and the tension over the Y2K problem made it evident that nearly everything of any significance in the future would depend heavily on computers, the internet, and English. So when I, a 26-year-old college teacher in Venezuela, saw a flier on a wall at the University recruiting teachers to "study computers and technology to enhance the learning process" in Hartford, Connecticut, I knew I'd found an opportunity.

After getting accepted into the Master's program, I traveled to the US for an intensive 4-month English course I was told would prepare me for the program. I had friends in Miami and Boston, but didn't want to be in a Spanish-speaking environment, so I chose to go to Denver, Colorado. There, I spent my time working hard and getting top marks. Soon, I realized I had drastically underestimated how difficult it would be to learn English at 27.

This realization came to me in a confidence-crushing experience at McDonalds. A friend and I went to field-test our language skills by ordering food. I memorized my order in advance and delivered my lines successfully at the counter. I felt great. The cashier then asked, "For here or to go?" I froze. I didn't prepare for this. I tried to remember my classes from the past months, and the only words I recognized were "here" and "go," so I assumed he was asking if I was from around here. "No, I'm from Venezuela!" I said. I could tell by the look on his face that it wasn't the answer he was looking for.

This small interaction made me realize that no matter how much I excelled at focusing on grammar, vocabulary, and memorization, I couldn't communicate in real-life situations. My Master's program was about to begin, so I needed a change of strategy.

The first thing I did was face my fear of communicating with native speakers. I did this by engaging in one-on-one conversations with a native English speaker friend who was willing to talk to me about whatever topic I was interested in.

I also worked hard on changing my mindset by consciously creating exposure to the English language by using it in my everyday life. Even with my Latino friends, I only spoke English. No matter how strange it felt or how long it took me to express an idea, I committed to this approach because my goal was to create a habit. I wanted English to become natural. And it worked. My confidence grew, and I was able to express myself in English.

In the Master's program, I became a teacher assistant. This position allowed me to talk with natives about more technical and language-specific topics, further deepening my knowledge and understanding of the world around me.

After graduating, I became a 4th-grade Spanish teacher in a two-way program in a Framingham, MA, public school, where I saw young students interact in a second language with ease and no fear of making mistakes or being ridiculed. They focused on communicating, expressing themselves, and getting their point across.

This experience became a turning point in my career and motivated me to get a second Master's Degree in Bilingual and Multilingual Education. These studies confirmed the importance of connecting with English in context.

Today, I communicate effectively in English and teach others how to do so as well with English 4 Life Network, the business I launched in 2019 to guide Latino professionals in gaining confidence and unlocking new personal and professional opportunities through immersive conversational experiences.

THE LEARNINGS

The problem I discovered while learning a second language, and I see it in my students as well, is that traditionally, languages, especially English, are taught as if the students were actors preparing to deliver lines on stage.

Good students memorize all the lines and wait for someone to speak the cue that will fit one of the responses they have ready. But when talking to people who haven't read the script beforehand, even the most dedicated student can freeze, just like an actor on stage who forgot their lines waiting for someone else to say the specific thing that will allow the conversation to continue.

But in real life, we don't memorize language. We use it. Conversations are not scripted; they're improvised, like jazz. In their native language, no one waits for someone else to say the right cue. We listen and then come up with the response on the fly.

When learning a new second language, they tell us to memorize vocabulary and grammar rules and assemble phrases in our heads before speaking them. But as children, we learn to interact with the language, to see it, hear it in context, and use it. Firstly, out of necessity, but later to connect to others and the world around us.

I'm convinced that the most effective way to learn is to practice with real people and in conversation to communicate and understand each other. Memorization can help a student acquire the tools to use a new language, but it is of limited use when applying it to something as simple as ordering a hamburger.

Human brains have mainly developed to make sophisticated communication possible. What I realized in my learning process was that when I focused on communicating my ideas during real conversations in real-life contexts – like discussing an article, asking for food in a restaurant, or making a point during a professional discussion – I learned how to communicate much more quickly than when I was trying to assemble sentences based on memorized vocabulary and rules of grammar.

This new mindset changed my experience and accelerated my results with much less conscious effort because I was immersing my brain in a stimulating environment and asking it to do the job for which it evolved – communicating with other humans.

THE INSPIRATION

I have been blessed to have a lot of exceptional role models throughout my life. One of the best sources of inspiration was my dad – an architect, teacher, and entrepreneur who addressed the need to increase housing for the disadvantaged in Venezuela by creating a prefabricated system that made new construction simple and inexpensive using local materials. The effort and creativity he used to solve problems in his personal and professional life inspired me to find goals I felt passionate about and find ways to overcome barriers to reach those goals.

Learning English was not one of my most efficient efforts, though I got a lot of help from teachers who focused on what students were trying to accomplish rather than their grasp of the entire language. The late college professor Rebecca Beke taught us to approach English strategically by identifying the key information in the text of important books written in English so we could understand the main ideas and the context in which they made sense. That technique turned out to be so powerful that I have adapted it to teach others using strategies to find key information in English songs, podcasts, videos, movies, and other media, just as she taught us to do with books and essays.

The difficulty I had in learning English using traditional methods at age 27 gave me a reason to believe the myth that adults can't learn a second language. One of my professors in the Linguistic Master's Program at UMASS Boston, the late Pepi Leistyna, helped shatter that myth using data from his research. He studied the relationship between language, culture, and experience. He stated that adults have developed a language and the ability to navigate the world and overcome obstacles. All they already know about the world in their native language helps them overcome the challenges of learning a second language and even enhance the process. Listening to him was inspiring, and I've used this approach in my teaching practices.

THE ADVICE

The best advice to those facing the challenge of living and working in the English-speaking world is to understand that it is possible as an adult to learn to communicate and express yourself in English as well as you do in your native language. The key is to remember you are trying to connect with and understand other people, not just memorize rules or vocabulary that may not reflect how native English speakers express themselves.

Be persistent, determined, and dedicated to pursuing your goal to speak with confidence. Don't worry about any mistakes you make. Mistakes are part of the process of learning a new language. Adults understand that and respect your effort, just as they forgive and even encourage kids to make similar mistakes as they learn to speak.

Make English part of your daily life, but remember that language learning is a lifelong process, not one you can complete and discard like a checklist. Once you are comfortable with the language, your English vocabulary will change as you pick up new colloquial terms, technical jargon, and slang through ordinary conversations. The first step is to help your brain, which is thinking in your native language 24/7, to think in English rather than simply translating. It will be frustrating at times, but every conversation brings you closer to your goal, and it will make every bit of effort worth it. It is like feeling the vibes of the language. Your understanding will grow once you begin hearing the language in your head.

Think of your goal not as "I want to learn fast" but "I want to communicate effectively." Linguists and neurologists break down the learning process into steps and analyze the characteristics of each, but that doesn't help them learn languages more quickly than it would help an athlete learn a new skill by reading about it.

Monitor your results, which seem to come slowly but are far more obvious to others, who are more generous in their perception of our abilities than we usually are ourselves.

THE PATH FORWARD

I believe in the power of language and the need to find solutions to the challenges we face in today's world. Most of the discussion leading to those solutions will be in English – the global language of business that is spoken by more than 1.5 billion people worldwide. That doesn't make learning English any less of a challenge but it does show how much greater your impact on the world can be if you can overcome your fears.

I hope in sharing my story that any adult including Latina immigrant professionals and entrepreneurs understand they can overcome the English barrier and do so confidently. It is not only possible but also very powerful to express yourself in English in the same way you do in your native Spanish.

It will help you grow, lead, and thrive in your personal and professional life, business, and community.

As I already said I learned English as an adult, and so have many others. I have also learned by connecting with many people, colleagues, and friends from different cultures, having personal and professional experiences that have helped me not only to improve my English but also expand my understanding of different points of view and find common ground to support others and create new opportunities for us and for others no matter who we may be.

My purpose with English 4 Life Network is to help fill the Massachusetts language gap, equipping Latino professionals, especially Latinas, with the English skills and confidence they need to grow, lead, and help their community thrive. Learning English has helped me thrive as a person, an educator, and now as a business owner. Today, I am committed to paying it forward, fostering an environment where everyone can flourish, develop, and succeed.

ABOUT LEONELA

Leonela Gonzalez-Fogarty is a Venezuelan-American with a Bostonian heart. She is an English Immersion teacher, linguistics, and the CEO of English 4 Life Network, a business that empowers Latino professionals and business owners to connect with the culture and maximize their possibilities by learning English through immersive conversational programs.

Leonela came to the U.S. in 1997 to pursue a Master's Degree in Educational Computing and Technology. She was 27 years old at the time and didn't know English. That experience was the first step in a lifelong connection with American culture and her pursuit to acquire English, which only deepened during the 23 years spent teaching language and cultural skills in multicultural environments at elementary, secondary, and professional levels in the U.S., Venezuela, Thailand, and Ireland.

Her passion for education brought her back to her adopted hometown of Boston in 2015. There, she began creating a unique learning method based on her experience and the techniques she learned in her Master's program in Bilingual and Multilingual Education. Leonela was proof that the myths about acquiring a language as an adult were untrue. Adults already have the cognitive skills necessary to achieve goals that require learning new topics, including a new language. She founded English 4 Life Network in 2019, and today she guides Latino professionals to gain the confidence they need to express themselves in English to grow their personal and professional opportunities.

Learn more and connect with Leonela at:
https://www.linkedin.com/in/leonela-gonzalez-fogarty-03493652/
https://www.instagram.com/english4lnetwork/
https://www.instagram.com/leonela_e4l/

LIZ CHALUISANT

"We are more than our job title, gender, ethnicity, accent, being a spouse, being a parent…WE ARE MORE THAN OUR OWN STORY"

- Liz Chaluisant

~ ~ ~

Liz Chaluisant is a driven leader with over 15 years of experience in diverse technical, business, and administrative domains. She currently serves as a Chief of Staff within the Department of the Navy (DON). In this role, she leads a team responsible for developing policy for analytical tools, crafting messaging for critical priorities, and designing rollout strategies for diverse research studies. She has received professional recognition for her work in STEM and Diversity efforts and enjoys spending her time mentoring the next generation of young Latinas through organizations such as United Latinas, Latina Engineer, Latin American Youth Center, and Step Up.

~ ~ ~

First, thank you, God, for this incredible journey. To my dear husband Jamar, your love and unwavering support are my foundation. To my precious sons Micah and Jacob, this chapter offers a glimpse into my heart, reminding you that you are capable of achieving anything you set your mind to. To my parents, Pedro and Sonia, you taught me the meaning of a healthy and nurturing love. To my siblings, Coralis and Pedro, my cheerleaders and confidantes, thank you for your laughter and love. And lastly, to my precious niece, Gianna, baby girl, remember this: the world awaits your unique brilliance, and I cannot wait to witness the amazing things you will achieve. This chapter is dedicated to each of you, with all my love and deepest gratitude.

WE ARE MORE THAN OUR OWN STORY

THE JOURNEY

I would like to take you on a little journey through the twists and turns that have shaped who I am today. When I started my career over fifteen years ago, I called myself "the only lonely." This is how I described my situation throughout my career, often finding myself as the only woman, the only Latina, and often, the youngest person in the room (well, not so young anymore). I grew up in San Juan, Puerto Rico, surrounded by a loving family and community. My parents instilled in me the values of faith, family support, and education as pillars for a successful life. In high school, I was not certain about my career path but hey, I went to a STEM school and loved math and science, so when I heard about chemical engineering, I was all in — Math? Check. Science? Check. A career that pays well? Triple check!

My original plan was to dive into the pharmaceutical industry after college, but things took a turn when Puerto Rico's economy started declining, and many pharmaceutical companies left the island. Therefore, I had two choices: finish my degree or start something new to help me get a decent career. I am not one to back down from a challenge, so I stuck it out and completed my degree. That is when my real journey began.

It is funny how opportunities knock when you least expect them. While interning at the Food and Drug Administration, a professor who was participating in an exchange program with the Department of the Navy, informed us about how they were seeking entry-level engineers. I always said I would only move to the United States if NASA called — well, close enough.

Oddly enough, I never had much exposure to military recruitment at my school; otherwise, I might have signed up! Taking a leap of faith, I submitted my resume and found myself in Maryland for an interview. Imagine me, with my imperfect English, sitting across multiple managers, nervously giving it my all. It was eye-opening to learn about the Department of the Navy's work and the myriad of opportunities for engineers like myself. To my surprise, I received a job offer within 24 hours. Suddenly, it was the summer of 2008; I just graduated, and boom! A job offer landed on my lap. What a blessing, right?

This new opportunity meant leaving everything behind – my house, family, friends, and community – and moving alone to the U.S. However, I got a job as an In-Service Engineer right out of college! My plan was to stay three years, polish up my English, and head back 'home' to look more appealing in the job market.

Change of plans - life loves to throw surprises. Here I am, still in the U.S., because, let us face it, God's plans are greater than mine. As Jeremiah 29:11 says, "I know the plans I have for you, declares the Lord, plans to prosper you and not to harm you, plans to give you hope and a future."

My career has not been a straight line; it has been filled with many detours, more like a twisting adventure. Some folks called me a "Unicorn" because I drifted from an engineer's usual path. Solving technical problems and using acronyms all day long sounded good at first, but seeing colleagues stuck in the same office corner for decades made me realize that I did not want that for myself.

Curiosity took the wheel, leading me to explore how my organization fit into the bigger picture. This opened my eyes to a whole new world! I saw myself more as a strategist and connector, so I decided to take a leap: I applied to a leadership program that allowed me to do a rotational assignment at the Headquarters level. My technical skills were top-notch, but I craved new challenges, and as an engineer, I was trained to solve problems. Beyond ensuring pilots could eject safely, what other problems could I solve?

I was accepted into the leadership program and was given an opportunity to transition to the program management field. Being at the Headquarters level brought up endless opportunities, new faces, and the chance to discover myself as a leader. A supportive boss pushed me beyond my comfort zone, sharpening my strategic thinking and leadership skills. He even trusted me to lead others, building my confidence to heights I never knew existed.

A mentor once told me, "Act like someone is always watching you." This struck differently during the leadership program's capstone project. A senior executive assigned as our project's champion was a silent observer who noticed my talent. After graduating from the program, a tap on the shoulder and a simple sentence changed everything: "Liz, I want you on my team." Shocked, honored, and nervous all at once, I was about to work for one of the Navy's top Senior Executives! Becoming his Action Officer was like a masterclass in true leadership. I saw integrity in action, respect for every expert, and genuine care for his team. This amazing chapter closed with his well-deserved retirement, followed by the world-altering curveball of COVID.

Over my life, change was the only constant. Thanks to the network I had built up, I landed a unique opportunity with the Marine Corps. Back in the technical realm, but armed with my strategic toolkit, I embarked on a new mission – crafting the strategic framework for the Marine Corps' chief engineer. Working with these brilliant minds pushed me further, making me question everything: Who was I? What was my purpose? Where was I headed?

Then, to my surprise, another door opened – diversity, equity, and inclusion (DEI). A whole new landscape, and I saw a chance to use my unique perspective as a Latina woman for good. Some doubted my choice, whispering warnings about career suicide, but their negativity couldn't drown out my heart. DEI became a reflection, pushing me to redefine success on my own terms.

Climbing the corporate ladder? Been there, done that, and proud of it. But today, success means finding your purpose and living it, balanced in mind, body, and spirit. I'm still on my journey, but I encourage you to ask yourself:

"What sets your compass spinning?" That, my friend, is the true north of success.

THE LEARNINGS

It was my very first week on the job—a new place, new faces, a different language, and freezing cold weather. I can vividly recall it as if it happened yesterday. Picture this: I was standing in a corridor surrounded by new colleagues, and out of the blue, this older gentleman strides up to me, points his finger, and says publicly, "Young lady, let me tell you something: you will never be successful... you're a woman, a Latina, and you speak with an accent." I stood there in disbelief, frozen in the moment. I had a choice to make: either let the tears flow or take it as a wake-up call, saying, "Hey Liz, welcome to your new adventure."

That very moment shaped my journey to where I stand today. It gave me strength, courage, and charted the course for what I aspired to be, realizing that I am more than what he said! I discovered that there are More than One who resemble me, talk like me, and think like me. I realized I meant More than One thing to many—I was hope for the women on the street, I was "competition" for the men sitting by my side, and I was the hero for the child I was raising. People were always watching me; they are always watching all of us!

I did not navigate these challenges alone. I had to build my tribe, support network, and Board of Advisors with mentors who saw me, believed in me, and taught me to embrace every part of who I am, including my accent—because it is part of my unique "brand."

Imagine being in a room full of future leaders, all confident and polished. But you are battling your inner critic, who is whispering about your accent in your head. Every word feels like a stumbling block, tripping you up with insecurity. During the leadership program, I was part of, I was paired with a coach, and one day, I shared my insecurities about my accent and how it made me feel like I did not belong. After one short pause, she said, "Write down the good things and not-so-good things about your accent." So, I began to scribble and let the words flow freely on the table, and what I saw surprised me. The richness of knowing two worlds balanced the awkwardness of switching tongues. The power to connect with people from different places matched the feeling of an outsider. Each "ugh" had a hidden "wow!" With her help and the advice of other mentors, I started to hear my accent differently. It was not a stumbling block; it was a secret superpower! This exercise unlocked something deeper: the power of my "two voices," the power of belonging.

Success means different things to everyone, and all I can say is that I feel blessed. I am healthy; my family, husband, kids, friends, and community stand by me in every aspect of my life. My determination to succeed started because of that one instance where someone told me I would not succeed because of who I am. What is the takeaway from this? We are more than what we see…better yet, let us declare this together – "I am more than what I see!" We are More than One of the labels society slaps on us. We are more than our job title, gender, ethnicity, accent, being a spouse, being a parent…WE ARE MORE THAN OUR OWN STORY!

THE INSPIRATION

One of my friends pointed out how, as Puerto Ricans, we learned to be resilient from a young age. Each year, we had to prepare for hurricane season, and if you know anything about Puerto Rico, the island has been hit hard by some big hurricanes. I recall the chaos when Hurricane Hugo struck. I found myself on top of the dining table with my baby sister while my parents fought to keep the water out. Then came Hurricane Maria, and seeing my family pull through tough times and come out even stronger reminded me how important it is to keep going, no matter what life throws at you.

Let me tell you, life has been no walk in the park, but I will say it again—I do count myself as blessed. During tough times, my faith has guided me through the uncomfortable seasons. I often tell people that there are two things that keep me going: Jesus and therapy.

As a Latina, my career path was shaped by noticing our community's scarcity of role models. Even though I knew they existed, I struggled to find a way to connect with them every time I searched. That realization ignited a fire, pushing me towards diversity, equity, and inclusion. I am determined to be a resource and champion for the younger generation within the Hispanic community.

Being Latina means understanding the unique hurdles such as the cultural details that shape our journey. I want to use my experiences to uplift and empower the younger generation. I aim to stand as a pillar of support, encouragement, and guidance for them along their paths.

THE ADVICE

Reflecting on my journey, there is some valuable advice I wish I could offer my younger self. I would encourage embracing my cultural heritage unapologetically. I would emphasize the importance of celebrating my identity and understanding that being Latina is a source of strength and resilience. I would speak up confidently, knowing my worth, and pursue my goals without hesitation.

For someone on a similar journey, I would emphasize the significance of building a supportive community. Find mentors and advocates to get guidance within and outside the Hispanic community; and nurture relationships with individuals who share similar experiences. We are better together! Surround yourself with positive people; it will eventually shift your mindset. I wish I had recognized this sooner!

You could say curiosity drives me - this is how I built my community and the circle of brilliant minds I call my Board of Advisors. I looked both inside and outside my organization for leaders who clicked with me and others with skills I wanted to learn. I imagined them as puzzle pieces fitting perfectly with my vision. I looked for professional organizations that shared my interests.

By becoming a member and volunteering, I surrounded myself with potential advisors and future friends. Sometimes, a simple "hello" goes a long way. I crafted messages on LinkedIn and emailed folks I admired, explaining my goals and desire to connect. Remember, even amazing people are approachable – just like you and me!

Bonus Tip: Never forget the power of "how bad you want it." Passion and drive attract opportunities like magnets. Building a community takes time and effort, but the rewards are endless. What is the worst that could happen? That they say "No"? Remember, even a "No" means "Next Opportunity." So, keep exploring, keep connecting. The rewards are worth the adventure!

I am also an advocate of practicing self-care rituals that bring joy. For me, it is going to church, working out, getting my hair and nails done, getting a massage, and going to therapy sessions. All of these have been pivotal for me in fostering self-awareness and personal development.

Moreover, I would advocate for exploring opportunities and the courage to step outside your comfort zone, as these experiences often lead to growth. We must embrace the idea that we are all a work in progress, foster a mindset of continuous improvement, and recognize that growth is a lifelong journey.

THE PATH FORWARD

My dear Sisters, Hermanas, this goes beyond merely having a seat at the table – I am here to encourage all of you to become Waymakers! Why, you ask? Because there are More than One of us, there are so many of us out there! We have the privilege and the responsibility to make way for others when there is no way and leave a trail for those who are coming behind us. The work we need to do and continue is like building a cathedral—we might not see it in our lifetime, but we are doing it because it is important for many generations to come.

Those of us who have stepped into these "exclusive spaces/rooms" must be determined to unlock them. Just holding the door is not sufficient; it is crucial that we keep it unlocked from within. Let us keep guiding the next generation with courage and an open mind without compromising who we are and our values. Therefore, what do you want this society to know about you? That you are more than what? This is your chance to fill in the blank!

ABOUT LIZ

Liz Chaluisant is a driven leader with over 15 years of experience in diverse technical, business, and administrative domains. She currently serves as a Chief of Staff within the Department of the Navy (DON). In this role, she leads a team responsible for developing policy for analytical tools, crafting messaging for critical priorities, and designing rollout strategies for diverse research studies.

Before being promoted to Chief of Staff in 2022, Liz served as the Chief Strategist for Marine Corps Systems Command's Chief Engineer and Deputy Commander for Systems Engineering and Acquisition Logistics. Her responsibilities included advising senior management on optimizing organizational structures, leading strategic planning efforts, and spearheading the restructuring of a Technical Authority framework.

Liz's civil service career began in 2008 at the Naval Surface Warfare Center Indian Head Division. Starting as an In-Service Engineer in the Systems Engineering Department, she managed procurement and in-service support for defense programs. Her career progressed within the DON, leading her to roles as an Assistant Program Manager overseeing workforce development initiatives and managing the Program Management College, and later as the Action Officer to the Executive Director of NAVSEA Warfare Centers. In this role, she provided strategic guidance to senior leadership, orchestrated digital transformation efforts, and integrated administrative and technical functions across 10 Warfare Center Divisions.

She is a graduate of the Polytechnic University of Puerto Rico where she earned a bachelor's and a master's degrees in chemical engineering and engineering management, respectively. She has received professional recognition for her work in STEM and Diversity efforts and enjoys spending her time mentoring the next generation of young Latinas through organizations such as United Latinas, Latina Engineer, Latin American Youth Center, and Step Up.

Learn more and connect with Liz at:
https://www.linkedin.com/in/lizchaluisant/

MARCY REYES

"We are not defined by the objects we own."

- Marcy Reyes

~ ~ ~

Marcy is an internationally recognized and awarded businesswoman and change maker with comprehensive skills in organizational leadership and over 20 years of experience in the fields of finance, education, and healthcare services. In 2017, Marcy founded The Financial Literacy Youth (FLY) Initiative serving over 3,500 individuals and is projected to provide programming to over 7,000 individuals by 2025. Marcy also serves as the Director of Market Strategy and Planning for CCA Health RI where she cultivates community awareness of and support for the CCA mission.

~ ~ ~

In dedication to my daughter, Katia Reyes, your presence is the beacon illuminating my world and infusing my life with purpose. Remember, you are destined for greatness.

A DOLLAR AND A DREAM

THE JOURNEY

I have a vivid childhood memory of trudging through the snow, grocery bags in hand, led by my mother, with my older sister and younger brother in tow.

Upon arriving at the grocery store, my mother, holding food stamps, looked at our cold faces and handed each of us a one-dollar coupon, urging us to pick out something we wanted. This seemingly simple act of generosity would later become a symbol of my early exposure to the value of money and resourcefulness. While my siblings eagerly rushed to the candy section, my selection process was meticulous. I found myself getting lost in the nuances of the combinations of various candies, seeking to optimize this single food stamp. During this moment, a visceral love of numbers began to emerge—a love that would significantly influence my future.

At age eight, I took a plane to visit my father for the first time since my early childhood. The summer spent with him, his wife, and our two new siblings was impactful, highlighting the stark difference in lifestyle between my father's lower-middle-class environment and the abject struggles of poverty at my mother's home. The return to my mother's home came with a harsh reality – we were poor, significantly so, a result of my mother's mental health challenges leading to the mismanagement of our finances.

The dichotomy between the comforts enjoyed during the summer months with my father and the dire circumstances at home with my mother began to shape my understanding of the importance of money.

As the desperate nature of our circumstances became more blatantly apparent, my brother and I were back in my father's custody within the year, but this time it was permanent. My life would change drastically from that point forward.

From the middle child of three to now being the eldest of four, my responsibilities grew. I assumed the role of maintaining the household, caring for my siblings, and contributing to expenses as I entered the workforce. The once-idealistic family environment gradually disintegrated over the years. Finances were mismanaged, domestic interactions became hostile, and peace was disrupted. The better life I was promised didn't materialize.

By the age of 17, I decided to venture off on my own, seeking independence from the tumultuous family dynamics. The subsequent years were a test of resilience, navigating through homelessness, poverty, and single motherhood with little resources and the poor money management skills inherited from my childhood. Often, we inadvertently repeat cycles because we never learned any other way.

In 2007, determined to break free from the cycle of poverty, I re-enrolled at the local college. This marked the commencement of my formal education, a beacon of hope amid adversity. As luck or maybe fate would have it, I enrolled in a finance class. Little did I know that this decision would be life-changing, not just in managing my own finances but in shaping my future mission. I graduated in 2012 with a degree in Finance and decided to continue on my academic journey.

In 2014, I graduated with my Master's Degree in Finance, armed with the knowledge and passion to make a difference. In pursuing my own growth and stability, I inadvertently became an advocate for financial education because it was at this juncture that I realized the transformative power of financial literacy. Armed with all the knowledge that I now had, I realized how many people's lives could be changed by understanding how to handle their own finances.

In 2017, I founded The Financial Literacy Youth Initiative, a non-profit organization dedicated to providing culturally responsive financial literacy programming to underserved and underrepresented communities.

Driven by a unique understanding of the challenges individuals from underserved communities face, I saw personal finance as a social justice issue. I firmly believe that everyone, irrespective of their race, ethnicity, or socio-economic background, should have access to personal finance resources. The initiative aims to equip individuals with the tools needed to change their financial and socio-economic futures, just as I had empowered myself to do.

My journey has been a testament to the power of education and personal growth. It underscores the belief that with determination, resilience, and access to essential resources, individuals can break free from the cycle of poverty and empower themselves to create a better future. Through my initiatives, I strive to share this belief with others, advocating for financial literacy as a catalyst for socio-economic change.

THE LEARNINGS

In the genesis of establishing The Financial Literacy Youth Initiative (FLY), a narrative unfolded against a backdrop of profound external and internal challenges. Beyond the intricate dynamics of childhood poverty and the complexities of single motherhood, an insidious adversary cast its shadow – imposter syndrome. It sowed seeds of doubt about my own capabilities and the prospect of attaining the level of performance to which I held myself accountable.

One significant memory stands out—the aftermath of teaching my inaugural personal finance class as an adjunct professor. There's nothing quite like the feeling of standing in front of a classroom of students and wondering if you are the right person to carry such an important message. I was charged with teaching them personal finance, but as such an important life lesson, it felt like a higher calling. What if I fail? What if they don't understand? What if someone else could do it better and affect the change I hope to make? Those echoes of self-doubt reverberated in my brain and had me questioning the efficacy of my influence on the lives of these students, leaving me cloaked in a profound sense of defeat.

In this vulnerable moment, seeking solace, I turned to my younger sister. Her response, filled with empathy, became an invaluable anchor. She not only empathized with my struggles, but also ignited a flame of resilience, encouraging me to persist. She insisted I give it one more try. This sisterly support served as a catalyst, propelling me to reassess and redefine my teaching approach with newfound determination. What could I do to really make sure these lessons stand out to students?

Invigorated, I embarked on a comprehensive reevaluation of the course curriculum. This metamorphosis delved deep into the realms of authenticity and connection. I decided to peel back the layers of my own personal financial journey, exposing raw challenges and triumphant moments. By bearing my personal financial narrative in the classroom, I sought to create an authentic connection with my students—a bridge between the theoretical concepts and real-world challenges they might encounter.

This shift yielded profound results, fostering a genuine connection and shared understanding within the classroom. The tears shed after that first defeated day were replaced by tears of triumph as I witnessed the empowerment on the student's faces. It wasn't merely an academic metamorphosis; it was a life-altering experience that extended beyond the confines of the classroom, permeating the lives of those I had the privilege to influence.

Simultaneously, within the broader canvas of my professional journey, creating a supportive ecosystem played a pivotal role. Colleagues and friends, passionately pursuing higher education and career advancement, emerged as pillars of strength. Their collective ambition for knowledge and professional growth became a driving force that laid the foundation for the inception of FLY. This shared pursuit of excellence became a defining moment, not only in my evolution but also in charting the trajectory for FLY's mission to empower underserved communities through financial education.

However, my story doesn't end here—it extends further into the realm of mentorship. Pivotal figures and seasoned mentors enriched my journey. Beyond imparting theoretical knowledge, their guidance was a wellspring of practical insights and strategic acumen. Their encouragement and wisdom became instrumental in navigating the complexities of establishing FLY. Their mentorship extended beyond the theoretical realm, offering practical insights, strategic guidance, and a nuanced understanding of the financial landscape.

Reflecting on the profound impact of having mentors, I've understood the immense value of seeking guidance from those with experience. One crucial lesson that stands out is mastering the art of asking for help and embracing mentorship. Initially, I hesitated to seek assistance, fearing it might reveal incompetence or weakness. However, with the unwavering support of my mentors, I learned that seeking help is not a sign of weakness but rather a demonstration of humility and a commitment to personal growth. This realization not only made me comfortable seeking guidance but also facilitated the development of meaningful connections with mentors who played a pivotal role in my personal and professional journey, allowing me to expand my business acumen quickly and effortlessly, benefiting from the collective wisdom and insights of those who had navigated similar paths before me.

One memorable anecdote that epitomizes the transformative power of mentorship occurred during a conversation with a close friend and mentor. As we discussed the importance of embracing diversity in thought and understanding others' paths, my mentor uttered a simple yet profound statement: "the world needs all sorts." These words resonated deeply with me, highlighting the significance of embracing different perspectives and approaches in leadership and decision-making. This perspective shift broadened my understanding of diversity and reinforced the notion that inclusivity is essential for fostering innovation and driving positive change. This insight has since become a guiding principle in my leadership approach, empowering me to create inclusive environments where all voices are valued and respected.

THE INSPIRATION

The journey of inspiration in my life has been a rich tapestry woven with threads of diverse influences ranging from personal connections to pivotal experiences, mentors, books, and evolving passions. In times of adversity, one of the earliest and most impactful inspirations was my younger sister. Her unwavering support and empathetic encouragement guided me during tough moments, propelling me forward in my mission to impart valuable financial knowledge.

Mentors have played an integral role in shaping my path. Their wisdom, practical insights, and nuanced understanding of the financial landscape were crucial in fortifying the importance of reshaping personal finance education. Beyond imparting theoretical knowledge, they provided strategic guidance, offering a blueprint for navigating the intricate journey of establishing the Financial Literacy Youth Initiative (FLY).

The transformative power of books and experiences has profoundly shaped my life journey. Their influence has etched lasting impressions, guiding me through moments of self-discovery and growth.

Amidst the vast array of literary treasures, several titles have shone brightly, each offering a distinct blend of wisdom and inspiration. "The Confidence Code" by Katty Kay and Claire Shipman stands out as a beacon of insight into the complexities of confidence. Its profound exploration has equipped me with the tools to nurture self-assurance and resilience, enabling me to confront challenges with poise.

Ibram X. Kendi's "How to Be an Antiracist" has ignited a fervent call to confront systemic racism actively. Kendi's candid reflections and thought-provoking analysis have spurred me into action, propelling me toward advocating for a more just and equitable society.

Lastly, "The Psychology of Money" by Morgan Housel has offered indispensable insights into wealth-building and financial security. Housel's astute observations have reshaped my approach to personal finance, empowering me to make informed decisions and debunk prevalent myths.

These literary treasures, among others, have left an indelible imprint on my journey, fostering personal growth, nurturing empathy, and equipping me with the resilience to navigate life's trials.

Reflecting on my past, I recognize how seemingly mundane moments have served as seeds of inspiration. Early trips to the store with my family amidst snowfall instilled a sense of collective resilience in me. My mother's unwavering generosity during challenging times planted the seeds of gratitude and perseverance within me. Later in life, witnessing the dedication of colleagues and friends to pursue education and career advancements spurred me to pursue my own academic endeavors.

As my journey unfolded, my sources of inspiration evolved, coalescing around the students of the FLY program. Their stories and experiences are a constant wellspring of motivation, fueling my determination to expand educational opportunities to underserved communities. Each success story validates the program's efficacy and serves as a catalyst for broader societal change.

Moreover, my passions find sustenance in the tireless efforts of leaders advocating for marginalized communities. Their collective endeavors to address systemic disparities inspire my commitment to reshaping financial education. Each leader's contribution to positive change reinforces the importance of collaborative efforts towards a more equitable future.

In essence, my journey is a tapestry woven with the threads of familial influence, personal experiences, and the profound impact of the FLY program's students. It is fueled by the collective wisdom of those who have paved the way and the relentless efforts of contemporaries striving for societal progress. With a deepened understanding and fortified commitment, I am driven by the belief in the transformative power of collective action, shaping financial education for the betterment of society.

THE ADVICE

Reflecting on my personal and professional journey, there are insights I would love to share with my younger self or with those navigating their own paths of transformation. At the core of my message lies the profound importance of resilience and self-belief. Understanding that challenges and moments of self-doubt are not indicators of failure but opportunities for personal and professional growth is a fundamental mindset to embrace early on.

Just as important is the recognition of the power of vulnerability. Opening up about personal experiences and embracing authenticity creates profound connections with others. This vulnerability fosters trust and establishes a shared space of understanding and empathy, allowing for a deeper and more meaningful connection with oneself and those around you.

Balancing confidence with humility is a delicate yet crucial aspect of personal and professional development. While confidence propels us forward, acknowledging that the learning journey is continuous cultivates a mindset of perpetual improvement. Every person you encounter on your journey has unique experiences to share. If you approach every interaction with an open mind and an eagerness to learn, you will be amazed at the connections you can create and what you will learn from them.

In the realm of habits and practices that have been instrumental in my personal and professional growth, the pursuit of feedback and mentorship stands out prominently. Actively engaging with mentors offering diverse perspectives and experiences has proven life-changing. These mentors, serving not only as guides but also as sponsors and coaches, played a crucial role in elevating my skills and helping me navigate challenges with wisdom and experience. I urge everyone to lean into your network of mentors and welcome the feedback they bring.

A habit I wish I had embraced more fearlessly earlier in my journey is the art of asking questions. Questions are not manifestations of weakness but rather gateways to understanding and growth. The cultivation of curiosity becomes a driving force for continuous learning, leading to a profound understanding of one's field and the broader landscape.

Recognition and celebration of your personal capabilities and achievements, no matter how minor or impressive, is much more important than you may think. Acknowledging what you have to offer helps build and sustain your confidence, which can provide the fuel you need when faced with challenges. There's a beautiful balance in being your own cheerleader and advocate while simultaneously understanding that a vast expanse of knowledge exists in the world that you can only hope to begin to uncover. Whatever your profession, it will be an ever-evolving landscape, so cultivating a humble mindset will keep you open to ongoing learning and adaptation.

It's also important to recognize that personal growth goes far beyond just your own individual growth. Growth doesn't happen in a vacuum. Establishing and nurturing a supportive community is a strategic imperative. Surrounding yourself with individuals who celebrate your achievements and align with your vision and mission creates a positive and empowering environment. There is nothing like being surrounded by supportive people who share your goals' excitement and are dedicated to contributing to your success.

I am a firm believer that sustained personal and professional growth is marked by the cultivation of resilience, the embrace of vulnerability, the balance between confidence and humility, the pursuit of feedback and mentorship, fearless curiosity, the celebration of personal achievements, and the intentional establishment of a supportive community. When woven together, these facets create a tapestry of growth, empowerment, and fulfillment.

THE PATH FORWARD

I aspire to leave a legacy that inspires others to recognize the transformative power of individual actions and to instigate change in the face of systemic injustice. My journey carries a message of empowerment and advocacy.

The legacy I hope to inspire is one where individuals, upon encountering systemic injustice, step into leadership roles and utilize their power to empower those who have been subjugated, repressed, and marginalized by existing systems. The world, as it stands, is not a product of impartial systems; rather, many established systems do not inherently support and elevate all people equally. My hope is that my legacy serves as a call to action, urging individuals to be the change they wish to see.

This call to action extends beyond passive observation of injustices, I encourage you to step up and actively engage in reshaping the systems that perpetuate inequality. Recognizing that true change often requires stepping out of our comfort zones and challenging existing norms; we need courage and conviction. You can use your voices, positions, and influence to advocate for those who cannot have a voice at the table.

Empowerment is at the core of the legacy I hope to leave. I believe every person possesses the capacity to effect change, regardless of their background or starting point. By sharing my story, I aim to ignite a spark in others, inspiring them to be champions for justice, equity, and empowerment.

I wish to shine a beacon of inspiration for others to navigate the complexities of systemic injustice. You have the agency to reshape the narrative and dismantle structures that perpetuate inequality. This is not merely a plea but an invitation to be proactive architects of change, leveraging your influence to create a more just and equitable world.

ABOUT MARCY

Marcy is an internationally recognized and awarded businesswoman and change maker with comprehensive skills in organizational leadership and over 20 years of experience in the fields of finance, education, and healthcare services.

In 2017, Marcy founded The Financial Literacy Youth (FLY) Initiative, a non-profit organization that provides culturally responsive financial literacy programming to underserved and underrepresented students; empowering youth with the knowledge, skills, and experiences to end generational poverty. Since the launch of programming in 2018, FLY has served over 3,500 individuals and is projected to provide programming to over 7,000 individuals by 2025.

As a Puerto Rican woman born into a family with little resources or support networks and over 20 years of experience in the areas of finance, education and healthcare, Marcy is uniquely suited to understand the challenges of the community she serves. She started her own academic career by putting herself through Rhode Island College and later received her Masters in Finance from Northeastern University.

In addition to her work with The FLY Initiative, Marcy serves as the Director of Market Strategy and Planning for CCA Health RI where she cultivates community awareness of and support for the CCA mission. With a keen focus on equity, inclusion, and innovation, Marcy is responsible for leading the development of the product portfolio, and product level growth targets, market strategies, and community partnerships.

Marcy proudly serves her community as a member of the Council on Postsecondary Education, on the Rhode Island Public Transit Authority (RIPTA) Board of Directors, as a member of the advisory council for Papitto Opportunity Connection, and as a Year Up mentor and educator.

Learn more and connect with Marcy at:

LinkedIn - https://bit.ly/MReyesLinkedIn
Website: www.flyinitiative.org

MARIA GONZALEZ

"Always stay fierce y nunca dar un paso atrás, ni para coger impulse"

- María Gonzalez

~ ~ ~

María is the Founder and Principal of M&A Supplier Diversity Consultants (M&A SDC). With over two decades of public sector experience, she is a dedicated and highly regarded consultant specializing in designing compliant supplier diversity programs and facilitating the diverse certifications of BIPOC businesses at both the federal and state levels. In recognition of her outstanding contributions and leadership, she was honored as one of the 2023 recipients of the Amplify Latinx 100 (ALX100) Awards, joining a select group of 100 exceptional individuals recognized for their achievements in Massachusetts.

~ ~ ~

This is dedicated to the memory of my mother, Ms. Adelina Feliciano, who, although small in stature, had the presence and attitude of a lion, my family, and to my ancestors, The Tainos.

FROM PIVOTAL MOMENTS TO INCLUSIVE IMPACT: MY JOURNEY OF RESILIENCE

THE JOURNEY

I am the product of a beautiful journey, shaped by pivotal moments, turning points, and a diverse background, all of which have influenced both my personal and professional experiences and made me the resilient human I am today.

Once upon a time, I drew my first breath in Puerto Rico, a small tropical paradise filled with captivating landscapes and rich cultural heritage. However, destiny had different plans for me. Raised in Arecibo on the northern side of the island, though born in Ponce on the southern side, I experienced the profound impact of my ancestral roots. Both sides of my family were deeply rooted in a lineage of coffee growers, a tradition that kindled my passion for the aromatic elixir that is coffee.

Growing up on our expansive farmland was an adventure of its own. Alongside my two younger sisters and baby brother, I savored the freedom to explore the bountiful expanse of nature, discovering its enchanting secrets and cherishing the bountiful gifts it bestowed upon us. Amidst the beautiful fields and the warm embrace of Puerto Rico's fertile soil, I developed a profound love for the land and learned to appreciate its blessings.

My father, a towering figure of immense strength, possessed a stern disposition that seldom allowed him to express praise or appreciation towards his children. Regrettably, his treatment of my mother and our family was cloaked in his abusive tendencies. Oddly enough, this unfortunate upbringing steered me towards the path of justice and protection.

Determined to make a difference, I began my journey as a police officer, dedicating many years to serving my community.

Amidst the turmoil of our family life, my courageous mother decided to liberate us from my father's grasp and set us on a path toward a better future. On a bitterly cold 1979 January night, we landed at Logan Airport, leaving behind the warmth of Puerto Rico for new opportunities in Massachusetts. I shall forever remain indebted for my mother's selfless act, as she granted us a chance to experience the true essence of a loving family.

Freed from the turmoil and chaos that had plagued our lives, we flourished in our new Massachusetts home. I graduated from Roxbury High School, my class being the last to graduate before the school closed its doors forever. With determination and a hunger for knowledge, I soared to the top of my class at the age of 17, paving the way for a brighter future.

Though life posed challenges, I pressed forward and obtained my college degree. Fate gifted me with the joy of motherhood, causing me to shelve my educational aspirations temporarily. Nevertheless, my relentless pursuit of knowledge persevered. In 2001, I rekindled my academic journey, proudly graduating from UMASS Boston, embodying the relentless spirit of resilience shared by countless single mothers. My thirst for knowledge and my strong desire to provide a better life for my boys pushed me further. Fueled by ambition, I resolved to chase my dreams until I held a master's degree in my hands.

In 2004, with unwavering determination and the encouragement of my loved ones, I triumphantly walked across the stage of Boston University, forever etching my name as the first college graduate in my immediate family. All this transpired while I worked tirelessly to support my family, raising three young boys as a single mother.

My interest in entrepreneurship was sparked at a young age when I observed the business prowess of my mother, Ms. Adelina, who sold home-cooked meals to farm workers and farm products such as milk, coffee, vegetables, and eggs in her neighborhood of Puerto Rico. This early realization demonstrated the power of providing for her family while making a positive impact.

In the grand tapestry of life, I found myself at the crossroads of single motherhood and a myriad of dreams. Raising my three boys, Darnel, Armany, and Gustavo, was a rollercoaster of obstacles, tears, and frustrations, but it did teach me to be a warrior. The driving force behind my relentless pursuit? The love for my trio – they were my North Star, a compass in the chaos. Balancing a full-time job, wrangling three boys, and chasing a college degree was like juggling flaming torches while riding a unicycle. Crazy? Absolutely. Worth it? Undoubtedly.

Fast forward to government work – fulfilling, yes, but there was always this itch, a dream of my own business simmering in the background like a good plot twist. And then, bam! My youngest son takes off for the real world, and I thought, "Why not retire and kickstart my own adventure?"

Now, five years down the road, and guess what? No regrets, just a heap of accomplishments and a truckload of life lessons. Life after the kids grow up is a whole new chapter – the sequel we didn't know we needed.

While establishing my own business, I faced challenges that taught me resilience and perseverance. These experiences deepened my passion for empowering others, specifically women and the BIPOC business community, fostering empathy toward those facing similar hurdles.

Positive experiences collaborating with like-minded individuals and witnessing the success stories of diverse suppliers solidified my belief in the power of diversity and inclusion, which fueled my drive to create lasting change in the business community.

However, I also have encountered resistance and skepticism from people resistant to change. Although frustrating, these setbacks actually provide valuable opportunities for me to develop strategies, refine my communication skills, and muster the courage to persevere. These lessons taught me the importance of adaptability, effective advocacy, and self-worth.

Over the years, I have realized that my background significantly influenced my path as an empowering changemaker. Growing up in a diverse community, I witnessed the benefits of inclusivity and developed a strong desire to dismantle barriers and create a level playing field for everyone. Guided by my mother's values of fairness, equality, and justice, I became committed to providing opportunities for underrepresented groups. Moreover, my experience as a police officer and working in the procurement sector equipped me with the necessary skills to effect change. I gained a comprehensive understanding of the challenges faced by diverse suppliers, enabling me to develop effective strategies and solutions with the belief instilled in me by Ms. Adelina: "De que si se puede y en esta vida no hay imposibilidades, solo obstaculos."

Let my journey be a reminder that single moms can be superheroes, balance is a wild ride, government gigs can fuel your passion, entrepreneurship is the spice of life, and life after kids? Well, that's the sequel where you become the badass protagonist of your own story. Face the difficulties head-on with the grit of a warrior and the wisdom of someone who's been there and done that. Your dreams? They're not just possible – they're inevitable.

No matter what curveballs life throws, you've got the power to slug 'em out of the park. With a dash of persistence and the right folks cheering you on, your dreams aren't just wishes; they're waiting to be snatched.

My path to where I am today has been shaped by pivotal moments and encompasses both positive and negative experiences. My experiences and challenges have helped me hone these skills and fuel my passion for diversity and inclusion. Through my work, I strive every day to create inclusive business environments and profoundly impact my community.

Life taught me that resilience knows no bounds. It taught me to seize every opportunity, fight against adversity, and never allow circumstances to dictate my future. Today, as I reflect on my journey from the coffee fields of Puerto Rico to the stage of entrepreneurship, I stand tall as a testament to the power of resilience, commitment, and indescribable love for my family and my little island of Puerto Rico.

THE LEARNINGS

As I reflect on my life, certain challenges are pivotal moments that have shaped who I am today. Two particular hurdles that tested my resilience were the insidious presence of racism and prejudices, as well as the relentless attempts made by others to discourage me from pursuing my business endeavors. These uphill battles required me to tap into my inner strength, resolve, and perseverance.

Prejudice can cast shadows on our lives, causing pain and hardship. In my journey, I have faced countless experiences of discrimination. Today, I share incidents that may resonate with many readers. Through these stories, I hope to inspire others with the message of resilience, self-acceptance, and the power of embracing our true selves.

Confronted with the need for home renovations, I contacted several contractors for quotes. Little did I know prejudice would taint this process. One contractor doubted my ownership and asked for proof, while another insisted on speaking to my non-existent "husband." However, refusing to settle for such treatment, I sought out a third contractor and found one that treated me with respect and secured my trust – and the job. The experience taught me the value of persistence and standing up against discrimination.

A routine trip to the local mall with my son unfolded into yet another encounter with prejudice. As we walked back to our car, our arms laden with shopping bags, a security guard approached and offered assistance. Baffled, I questioned his intent. It was then that he pointed out our apparent dissimilarity (my son identifies as an Afro-Latino and is very proud), leaving my son devastated. While his tears broke my heart, it fueled my resolve to teach him an invaluable lesson. I reminded him always to walk tall and be proud of who he is, regardless of others' narrow-minded assumptions.

These experiences became catalysts for personal growth, awakening my inner strength and igniting a passion for driving change. Empowered by my voice and fueled by empathy, I vowed to share my story, empower others who have suffered injustice, and work towards creating a more inclusive world. Together, we can challenge biases and embrace diversity, fostering a society that celebrates the uniqueness of every individual.

Racism and prejudices have shown up in various aspects of my life, subtly challenging my self-worth and limiting my opportunities. I often found myself facing discriminatory remarks or biased treatment, which left me questioning if I could truly achieve my goals. However, I refused to let these obstacles define me or determine my worth. Instead, I chose to draw from the love and inspiration I received from my loved ones, friends, and mentors.

To overcome the negative impact of racism and prejudices, I embraced a strategy of self-empowerment. I educated myself about the historical struggles of marginalized communities and gained a deep understanding of the systemic obstacles I was up against. Armed with knowledge, I sought to challenge stereotypes and misconceptions, proving that my abilities and dreams were not defined by the color of my skin or the biases of others.

Moreover, I honed my coping mechanisms, finding solace in helping others who were and still are facing these same challenges, which allowed me to channel my frustrations into something positive, fueling my resolve to soar above the constraints imposed by societal expectations.

However, the battle wasn't solely against external forces. There were also countless instances when well-meaning people in my life tried to dissuade me from pursuing my business aspirations. They doubted my chances of success and feared I would face unnecessary hardships. Yet, their doubts only fueled the fire within me. I found the inner strength to persevere, driven by my unyielding belief in my abilities and my relentless desire to prove them wrong.

I found that I didn't have to navigate these challenges alone. I surrounded myself with a support system of like-minded individuals who shared my entrepreneurial spirit. These mentors, friends, and fellow entrepreneurs became beacons of inspiration and encouragement during moments of doubt. Their guidance and belief in my vision provided the necessary boost to keep pushing forward, even when the seas seemed a bit rough.

As I faced these challenges head-on, I realized the importance of challenging established norms and disrupting the status quo. I refused to conform to preconceived notions of success, choosing instead to carve my own path. In an industry riddled with stereotypes and rigid expectations, I pushed boundaries and embraced innovation, challenging the traditional norms that hindered progress.

A moment that stuck out was when I was informed that succeeding in the realm of supplier diversity within my new business would be challenging due to the various existing agencies dedicated to supporting the business community. This perspective was offered by an individual within the federal government. While expressing genuine gratitude for their advice, I emphasized that certain agencies may lack the essential cultural comprehension required to assist the BIPOC community, which I possess effectively and can readily share in a language that resonates with them. I now serve as a coach and trainer with several non-profit organizations that are advocates for the BIPOC business community of Massachusetts.

This journey was anything but easy. But through it, I discovered my true strength and resilience. Each challenge was an opportunity to rise above to showcase my character's strength and unyielding spirit.

So, dear reader, when confronted with obstacles, be it racism, prejudices, or naysayers, remember that your worth and potential are immeasurable. Draw upon your inner reservoir of strength, utilize effective coping mechanisms, and seek out a support system that lifts you higher. Embrace the courage to challenge established norms and disrupt the status quo, for it is in defying expectations that true greatness is achieved. Let your journey be an inspiration to others and a testament to the indomitable spirit within us all.

THE INSPIRATION

Throughout my life, I have been fortunate to find inspiration that guides me during difficult times and ignites my passion. My three sons, Darnel, Armany, and Gus, have been a constant source of motivation. Witnessing their growth, resilience, and ability to overcome obstacles has instilled in me a genuine desire to become the best version of myself.

Moreover, my grandchildren - Elijah, Aliyah, and Isaiah - have brought a new purpose into my life. Seeing the world through their innocent eyes has reminded me of the importance of making a lasting impact on future generations.

My sisters' steadfast love and support have played an instrumental role in shaping my journey. Their strength, resilience, and belief in me have been a guiding light, propelling me forward when challenges seemed insurmountable.

Additionally, the transformative presence of my life partner, George, has been pivotal in my life. Their unconditional love and constant encouragement have given me the courage to chase my dreams and confront adversity with resilience.

Lastly, the countless strong and outspoken Latinas who have graced my path have inspired me to embrace my heritage and LATINIDAD, stand up for justice, and strive for greatness. Witnessing their unrelenting perseverance and powerful voices constantly reminds us how we, as individuals, can affect meaningful change.

As my journey progresses, my inspirations continue to evolve. Each experience, encounter, and lesson learned shapes my perspective and intensifies my passion. Even during moments of uncertainty, I am reminded of the incredible individuals who have touched my life, fueling my inspiration. They serve as a vivid testament that strength, love, and determination can conquer any obstacle we encounter.

THE ADVICE

Reflecting upon my previous professional experiences as a dedicated police officer and a public employee with the Commonwealth of Massachusetts, I am compelled to offer guidance to my younger self and to individuals navigating a similar journey. These experiences have shaped my perspective and instilled in me invaluable insights that I wish to convey, guided by my acquired wisdom.

I would impart advice to my younger self to embrace the power of self-compassion and balance. In the demanding roles I have held, it is easy to become consumed by the pressures and expectations placed upon us. I now recognize the importance of nurturing one's well-being, both physically and mentally. Encourage yourself to take moments of respite, engage in activities that bring joy and fulfillment, and prioritize self-care. Doing so will recharge your spirit, enhance resilience, and be better equipped to serve others effectively.

I learned that believing in humanity and being empathic as a police officer and public servant is vital to recognize that unique circumstances, struggles, and aspirations shape every individual we encounter. By embracing empathy, we can foster genuine connections with others, bridge gaps in understanding, and cultivate a more compassionate and inclusive society. Approaching every interaction with an open heart and a desire to understand fosters trust and forge meaningful relationships.

I advise young entrepreneurs and peers to nurture a growth mindset that thrives on continuous learning and adaptability. Embrace every opportunity to expand your knowledge base, hone your skills, and broaden your perspective. Seek mentors who can guide and offer wisdom gained through their own experiences. Embrace constructive feedback as an opportunity for growth, recognizing that personal and professional development is ongoing. In times of difficulty, remind yourself of the impact you can have on individuals and communities, and let that drive you forward.

Several habits and practices have been instrumental throughout my career in fostering personal growth. The first, regular self-reflection, has allowed me to gain clarity on my values, strengths, and areas for improvement. It has allowed me to assess my actions, learn from my mistakes, and evolve as a person. Additionally, active listening has become a transformative habit. By truly hearing and understanding the perspectives of others, I have cultivated deeper connections and fostered collaboration and harmony in the workplace. Lastly, maintaining a commitment to lifelong learning has been pivotal. Through continuous formal or informal education, I have enriched my understanding of diverse perspectives and expanded my skill set, making me more effective in my roles.

THE PATH FORWARD

As a Latina advocate and a resilient woman of a certain age, I aspire to cultivate an enduring legacy that resonates with others through the narrative of my journey. I desire to impart the profound message that the passage of time should never constrain one's capacity for continual growth, impactful contributions, and triumphs.

I extend a compelling call to action, urging individuals, especially a Mi Gente Latina, to wholeheartedly embrace their distinct identities, ardently champion the well-being of their communities, and purposely dismantle any societal barriers that may seek to impede their progress.

Let our collective commitment be a catalyst for change, fostering a future wherein age, gender, race, ethnicity, religious beliefs, sexual orientation, gender identity, or background cease to be restrictive factors, liberating individuals to realize their aspirations and effect profound positive change in the world.

Together, let us forge a path toward a future where the shackles of societal limitations are dismantled, allowing the brilliance of each individual to shine unencumbered.

ABOUT MARIA

María is the Founder and Principal of M&A Supplier Diversity Consultants (M&A SDC), a consultancy firm recognized for its industry leadership. She is a dedicated and highly regarded consultant with over two decades of public sector experience. Leveraging her expertise, María specializes in designing compliant supplier diversity programs and facilitating the diverse certifications of BIPOC businesses at both the Federal and State levels.

Previously, María was pivotal in the Commonwealth of Massachusetts, specifically within the Operation Services Division. During her tenure, she provided invaluable support to small and diverse businesses, offering certifications, procurement workshops, and tailored coaching. Her efforts transformed over 1,000 small businesses and nonprofits, equipping them to effectively market themselves to the state and its agencies.

María later transitioned to the Executive Office of Administration & Finance, where she made significant contributions to policies and procedures that improved the lives of the Commonwealth's residents and business owners from her position at the State House. In addition to her primary roles, María generously volunteers as a Certified SCORE Business Counselor for the SEMA chapter. She also holds key positions on the Board of Directors for the TACC and serves as an Advisory Committee Member for the Bristol-Plymouth Regional High School. María's commitment to advancing women's status is evident through her role as a Commissioner for the Bristol County Commission on the Status of Women.

In recognition of her outstanding contributions and leadership, she was honored as one of the 2023 recipients of the Amplify Latinx 100 (ALX100) Awards, joining a select group of 100 exceptional individuals recognized for their achievements in Massachusetts. Originally from Puerto Rico, María established her family's residence in Boston before relocating to Taunton in 2001. In her leisure time, she tends to her garden, indulges in literature, enjoys eclectic music, takes daily walks, and expresses herself through Salsa dancing. Notably, María is the sole vegetarian within her close-knit family circle.

Learn more and connect with María at:

linkedin.com/in/masdc2019
supplierdiversityconsultants.com

MARIA JIMENEZ

"Always stay fierce y nunca dar un paso atrás, ni para coger impulso!."

- Maria Jimenez

~ ~ ~

Originally from Peru, Maria is a seasoned, bilingual finance and accounting professional with an MBA. She has experience in the private and the nonprofit sectors, holding senior management positions and leading teams in Latin America and the U.S. For the last five years she has worked at Your Part-Time Controller (YPTC), where she serves as a financial advisor and Controller for nonprofits in WDC. Maria is committed to advancing equity, diversity, and inclusion in the workplace; and she is passionate about women empowerment.

~ ~ ~

I would like to dedicate this chapter to my mom who lived her life in service to others. She is my angel now. To my father for being an inspiration for me. And my husband for his love and support always.

EMBRACING CHANGE: THE CATALYST FOR PROFESSIONAL AND PERSONAL GROWTH

THE JOURNEY

I am a proud Peruvian and American citizen. I am the product of divorced parents; I have a loving mother and a smart, over-achieving father. We lived in Mexico for two years while my father studied for a Master's in economics, and my mom took care of my little brother and me. After the divorce, my mom, brother, and I stayed in Peru, where I lived for many years.

My parents clearly influenced my upbringing. My mom was the kindest person I have ever met. She gave all she could to anyone in need. My father taught me the importance of education, perseverance, and hard work. We did not have much money but were fortunate enough to meet our basic needs.

During my younger years, my nation faced the impact of one of Latin America's most destructive terrorist organizations, known as the Shining Path. This group aimed to overthrow the government using violent tactics, causing widespread suffering and loss of lives during the 1980s and 1990s. I could not imagine the repercussions these events would have on my generation. It was a sad and dark period for Peru. However, the experience also taught me about resilience and community and the ability to endure individual and collective hardships. The Peruvian government, together with the army and peasant rounds "rondas campesinas," worked tirelessly to counter the Shining Path. They eventually reduced their influence and brought some relief to the affected communities. Unfortunately, people are still waiting for the reparations recommended by the Truth and Reconciliation Commission in Peru.

Education has always been very important to me. I studied accounting at the Catholic University in Peru and received a Master's in Business

Administration (MBA) from EGADE Business School in Mexico. My professional journey started in the for-profit sector in Peru, and then, searching for a more meaningful career, I transitioned to the nonprofit sector. My career in the nonprofit sector allowed me to travel overseas, work in different countries, learn from different cultures, and work here in the United States.

In the nonprofit sector, I started as a Finance Officer at the SNV Netherlands Development Organization. I worked very hard and developed a great work relationship with the Head of Administration of Latin America. Because of her, my work was noticed, and sure enough, when a position opened, the deputy regional director promoted me to the sub-regional finance manager of Central America. My position was based in Honduras, and my responsibilities continued to grow.

The organization faced significant financial stress in 2011, and the SNV Head Office decided to cut the funding to Latin America and focus on Africa and Asia. I needed to learn to adapt quickly and motivate my staff. It was a difficult time for me but also a wonderful opportunity; I grew professionally, learned how to manage a finance department in uncertain times, increased my knowledge about international development and multilateral organizations, and grew my network. Finally, when my position disappeared, I found myself at a crossroads.

I made the difficult decision to move to the USA and find a job in an international nonprofit. Because of my network in Central America, I learned that there were many international nonprofit organizations headquartered in Washington, DC. While I'd heard that obtaining a work visa in the US wouldn't be easy, I didn't let that stop me. I contacted my former Deputy Regional Director, the American woman who had promoted me at SNV Latin America. She introduced me to the executive director of the SNV USA organization, and soon, they hired me.

However, my career was not a straight line. I transitioned to a local Latino nonprofit to help entrepreneurs a few years ago. Since then, I have continued strengthening my involvement with the Latino community in Washington, DC. I started Women in Business, a Latina women's network in Washington, DC, as a co-founder with other powerful Latinas.

In 2018, looking for more balance in my life, career, and work in the community, I applied for a job at Your Part-Time Controller (YPTC), where I use my finance and accounting skills to support nonprofits and help my Latino community. At YPTC, I have served as Controller for six nonprofits in Washington, DC. I have collaborated with different departments/areas. Now, I help my organization to grow and support the U.S. Hispanic nonprofit market.

I have developed a strong commitment to Diversity, Equity, and Inclusion. I started the 'Latinas at YPTC' group. This group brings Latino women in the company together to connect personally and professionally, supporting our sense of belonging in the workplace. I went on to join the YPTC Equity Committee as co-chair and a subcommittee member, and I started an initiative to create other ERGs in the company.

I am grateful for my ever-evolving journey because I learned the importance of pursuing my dreams, embracing change, and living my purpose.

THE LEARNINGS

During my career journey, I learned the importance of embracing change and trying new things. I transitioned my career three times. First, I moved from the for-profit sector to the nonprofit sector. Then, I decided to move from finance to programs within the nonprofit sector. In 2018, I transitioned back to the for-profit sector with YPTC, which focuses on nonprofits, which is the best of both worlds for me. Change often happens beyond our control, which becomes a great learning opportunity to embrace it.

Towards the beginning of my career, I was laid off. I felt ashamed even to tell anybody. Instead, I drew on all of my inner strength to get out of that situation. I returned to being a part-time assistant teacher at the university while looking for another job. I took the time to do self-reflection about what I wanted to do next and then focused on applying for those kinds of jobs. Looking back, I am grateful I was laid off at such a young age because that experience taught me an important lesson: everything changes, and nothing is permanent, but I can choose how to respond.

The most pivotal moment in my career occurred when I was working in Central America, and as I mentioned before, my position disappeared. I found myself at a crossroads, but I was more conscious that something good would happen out of that situation, having learned from my previous layoff experience that there are gifts to be found in even the hardest situations. I decided to follow my heart to move to the USA alone and with only two bags. I not only found a job, but I also met my husband. It was such a great life lesson for me: follow your dreams, listen to your body (in my case, my heart), be positive, say what you want, cultivate your network, and great things will happen. I'd like to add that I recognize the privilege of being able to come to this country in this way.

The most difficult struggle I have ever faced was learning to manage stress and avoid burnout. I have experienced burnout on several occasions throughout my twenty-five-year career. I have learned the hard way the importance of self-care and self-awareness. Every setback taught me something I used the next time, and the process continues. There are so many lessons in my struggles; each gives me a deeper understanding of myself and the world around me.

I also have tried a variety of coping strategies, but I've found that returning to my body helps me the most. I have done this through yoga, meditation, Zumba, and more recently, Biodanza. Using my body as a tool to cope with life stressors has been a life-changing realization, and I urge you to try it and find what works for you!

Another great life-learning experience was to develop a support system around me. As an immigrant, it was imperative for me to build those support systems through friendships and networks for women. One barrier I encountered was being the only woman in the room in work meetings. Having more women in leadership positions benefits all of us. We can access sponsors, mentors, and allies that will help us to grow in our careers. Experiencing these deep connections allowed me to disrupt the status quo by building up and supporting Latina women, which has been overwhelmingly rewarding. I feel like I have found my true purpose in life: supporting and empowering women, particularly Latino women.

I have become the sum of all of my experiences, some that I called 'negative situations' at the time, but now I am grateful for them because they made me who I am today.

THE INSPIRATION

When I think of who and what has inspired me over my life, I'm filled with gratitude for the length of that list.

My biggest influence is my parents. My mom modeled the importance of giving to others, shifting how I approach my life and career. On the other hand, my father has been an inspiration from his humble beginnings to obtain a Ph.D. in Economics from a university in the US. Anything is possible with hard work and perseverance!

My husband is a source of motivation and helps to keep me grounded. He is a dedicated professional working in the Philanthropy sector. He also has my back when times are difficult; I am grateful for that.

I am lucky enough to have a handful of individuals outside my family who supported and motivated me during my career journey. They are my friends, mentors, my sponsors, and allies. As mentioned earlier, some of them opened doors for me to get a job in the US. Others support and motivate me in my work to empower Latino women.

My inspiration has evolved throughout my journey. For the last twelve years, certain people and books have inspired me in my career and life. One of them is The Blue Sweater by Jacqueline Novogratz. She disrupted the social sector with her manifesto about "moral imagination: the humility to see the world as it is, and the audacity to imagine the world as it could be. It's having the ambition to learn at the edge, the wisdom to admit failure, and the courage to start again." (https://acumen.org/manifesto/)

I was also impressed by the work and the books of Zainab Salbi - Between Two Worlds and Freedom Is an Inside Job - she is a founder, a journalist, and a celebrated humanitarian. Another must-read author for me is Brene Brown. I really enjoy and learn much from her books: the Gifts of the Imperfection, Dare to Lead, and Atlas of the Heart.

I am also inspired by Dolores Huerta and her work as a Latina community organizer. I was excited to meet her in person in late 2023.

I must confess I get motivated and inspired the most when I am in a room with smart and powerful women. I belong to several networks here in the US: Women Together, Women in Business, Latinas at YPTC, United Latinas, and Women of ALPFA (Association of Latino Professionals for America). When I worked as a program business coach to support Latino entrepreneurs, I was in awe of the Latina entrepreneurs' stories of grit, resilience, and perseverance. They were truly an inspiration and the reason I decided to co-found a Women in Business network.

I am an enthusiastic listener of Ted Talks and podcasts. The newest podcasts I am enjoying are "A la Latina," hosted by Claudia Romo Edelman and Cynthia Kleinbaum (for Latina professional women), and "Sh*t I just quit my job" hosted by Maricella Herrera (for anyone in a transition) and the "Anxious Achiever" by Morra Aarons-Mele who talks about the intersection of work and mental health.

Because of all of them, I got to know myself more, focus on my strengths, embrace change, and live my purpose.

THE ADVICE

I want to share some advice with you that I wish somebody had given to me when I was younger:

1. **Self-care should be our priority number one**. I shared earlier that I learned the hard way the importance of self-care. In my experience, always returning to my body helped me the most because I could be self-aware of what was happening inside of me and take better care of myself. And this takes practice.

2. **Change is good and constant, so do your best to embrace it.** Change is one of the greatest things that can happen for us. For instance, changing industries, sectors, or areas within your organization will give you the skills you need to grow professionally, and you can always apply what you learn in your next role. Additionally, moving to different countries will give you cultural competence skills that will enrich your career and life. If you have an opportunity to take a job in a different state or a different country, do it!

3. **Take risks and follow your dreams.** In doing that, think positively and speak out loud about what you want to the universe. Cultivate your network, and great things will happen. I guarantee you that, but also that you will experience failure at some point in your life as well. The most important part is learning to see what failure is teaching us. It is easier to say it than to do it. One tip is to write down your lessons learned in a journal and return to your notes whenever needed.

4. **Do what you love, and find your passion.** One way to discover your passion is through self-reflection. Spending some time with yourself is important in developing a meaningful life and career. It will help you to grow as a person. Think about the activities that you enjoy doing. Tracking all of this in a journal is a good idea, too. Having a life or career coach will help you with this process.

5. **Always remember that building relationships is as important as working hard**. You will find mentors, sponsors, allies, and longtime friends through those relationships. It is crucial to expand your network. Early in my career, networking was not a known practice. I learned the importance of networking over time. I suggest joining professional industry associations, a university alumni network, women's networks, or

meet-up groups. I will suggest some women's networks at the end of the chapter. Having networks will help you with self-confidence and feel empowered. Be strategic when you select your network to experience the power of community, the importance of supporting each other, and celebrate achievements together! Also, be intentional when you expand your network. I say that because you can build your own Personal Board of Directors. This is a great strategy to advance your career. Your Board can consist of 5-8 people you can contact for advice about your career, e.g., transitions, salary negotiation, promotions, etc. It is recommended to have a Sponsor – a person who is two levels up from you in their career, a mentor, a coach career, an ally, a college or university professor, a friend who knows you very well, and a family member who has a professional career. You may also want to have a diverse Personal Board of Directors, people from different industries, backgrounds, race, age, etc. Also, I'd love to share these helpful articles:

- 4 Steps To Build a Personal Board of Directors (Because You're the CEO of your career)[1]
- The 5 people you need on your 'personal board of directors,' according to a careers expert (CNBC)[2]

6. **Finally, I want to share with you that having a positive attitude – a smile- and listening to others with empathy are the two secrets in life.** Empathy will help you understand diversity, equity and inclusion, which are important in the workplace and our society.

THE PATH FORWARD

The first thing to achieve success in life is to know ourselves. Spend time with you. Practice self-reflection to know your strengths, weaknesses, and your purpose: why you are here. Then, focus on your strengths and live your purpose.

---

(1) https://www.linkedin.com/pulse/4-steps-build-personal-board-directors-because-youre-szakal-mraes/

(2) https://www.cnbc.com/2022/04/04/the-5-people-you-need-on-your-personal-board-of-directors-according to-a-careers-expert.html

If you are a woman of color or a Latina who wants to do more with your life, please remember we are social beings; we need a support system around us to have a sense of belonging. Consider starting or joining a women's network group that focuses on your interests and will help you grow professionally and personally. When women are together, amazing things happen!

Here are some networks you may consider joining; many of them have great free resources.

- Ellevate Network
- Lean In Circles
- United Latinas
- Women in Business
- Women of ALPFA
- Women Together
- #WeAllGrow Latinas

As Latinas or women of color, it is very important to understand the concepts behind diversity, equity, and inclusion. Educate yourself about unconscious bias, cultural competence, and inclusive leadership so that you can use tools to navigate the corporate world or any sector where you work.

Consider joining an employee resource group (ERG) in your organization. If you do not have one, then you can start one. Do not do it alone! Start a founding committee and invite other people to join you. Creating a vision for the group and connecting with ERG leaders in other companies is very important.

Finally, live your life with authenticity! Do not be afraid to be you. You can be a great change-maker in everything you do and an inspiration for others! I am sure you will be.

ABOUT MARIA

Originally from Peru, Maria is a seasoned, bilingual finance and accounting professional with an MBA. She has experience in the private and the nonprofit sectors, holding senior management positions and leading teams in Latin America and the U.S. For the last five years she has worked at Your Part-Time Controller (YPTC), where she serves as a financial advisor and Controller for nonprofits in WDC. Her curiosity brought her to join the YPTC sales department and collaborate with other areas like Strategic Partnerships and Talent Acquisition. For her, the most satisfying aspect of the work with nonprofits is helping with finance and accounting so the clients may focus on their mission to improve lives in the US and abroad.

Maria is committed to advancing equity, diversity, and inclusion in the workplace. She has been working with the YPTC Equity Committee as the Equity co-chair and on various subcommittees. She founded and led the employee resource group' Latinas at YPTC' and is currently a co-chair of the group, which has a vision to create a safe space for Latinas, to be supportive with each other and act as a voice for Latinas at YPTC. María was awarded the 2022 YPTC Equity Award.

Maria is passionate about women empowerment and volunteers with various Latino women organizations. She is a member of the Women of ALPFA (Association of Latino Professionals for America) Strategic Development (National) Committee where she seeks to advance Latino professional women in the workplace. She is a co-founder of Women in Business, a Latina entrepreneurs' network in WDC, where she co-developed a Latina entrepreneurs' virtual program during the pandemic. She is a member of United Latina network and an enthusiastic author contributor to the Extraordinary Latinas Volume III book. For her work in the community, she was awarded the 2023 Peruvian Expat Award for Excellency.

Over the last few years, Maria has been a speaker at different events and conferences. She loves sharing her knowledge and experiences as a way to give back to the community. Maria studied Accounting at the Catholic University of Peru, and then received an MBA in EGADE Business School in Mexico.

She enjoys walking with her husband, dancing to Latin music, and practicing biodanza.

Learn more and connect with Maria at:

https://www.linkedin.com/in/maria-jimenez-mba/

PAULE VALERY JOSEPH

"I have realized that our imperfections are not something to hide, but aspects of our identity that contribute to our strength and character."

\- Paule Valery Joseph

~ ~ ~

Paule V. Joseph, Ph.D., MBA, MS, FNP-BC, FTCNS, FAAN, is a renowned Venezuelan-American nurse scientist and clinician who has markedly impacted chemosensory (taste and smell) science, genomics, and precision health. With over 100 publications, she is a recognized figure in sensory science research. Her work has been showcased in top-tier academic journals and captured the attention of the media, such as TIME, NPR, and the New York Times. She has been honored with multiple awards and recognitions for her work from several institutions and global organizations. In addition, she mentors and fosters inclusivity, especially for underrepresented individuals and women in science.

~ ~ ~

To the indomitable spirit of curiosity and resilience that dwells within us all. This chapter is imbued with my deepest gratitude and love, dedicated first and foremost to God and my family. To my parents, whose sacrifices laid the foundations of my dreams, instilling in me the courage and perseverance to chase those dreams. To my sister, whose unwavering support and joy lighten up the darkest days, teaching me the power of faith, laughter, and resilience. To my partner, Dr. Hugo Tejeda, your love and wisdom are a guiding light. To my stepsons, Caleb and Noah, thank you for embracing me with open hearts and showing me the boundless joy of family and the wonder seen through your eyes. You remind me daily of the reasons we strive to better the world around us. I extend this dedication to my mentors, whose guidance and wisdom have been invaluable on my journey. Your belief in my potential, especially in moments of self-doubt, has been a guiding star. To my friends and colleagues, who have become family, your friendship and shared passion for discovery have greatly enriched my life. I hope my career, which embodies the fusion of cultural heritage, grit, and faith with scientific achievement and inspires you to take the road less traveled. It is a testament to the idea that our backgrounds, no matter how humble, are springboards for incredible feats and societal contributions. To you, the reader, joining me on this narrative adventure, I wish these pages inspire you to embrace your heritage and stories as pillars of strength. May my journey encourage you to see the potential within yourself to bridge different worlds, blending the richness of your past with the boundless possibilities of the future.

With heartfelt sincerity,
Dr. Paule Valery Joseph

FROM CULTURAL ROOTS TO SCIENTIFIC BREAKTHROUGHS: A JOURNEY OF PURPOSE, PRIDE AND IMPACT

THE JOURNEY

The journey I have undertaken as a changemaker is shaped by my personal history, cultural heritage, and the profound experience of caring for a loved one with a rare disease. Born in Venezuela with Haitian roots, my life has been a blend of diverse traditions and a relentless quest for knowledge. My parents emphasized the importance of education and hard work, values that have guided me through numerous challenges.

From a young age, I discovered my calling to serve. As a child, I always sought opportunities to help and serve others. Therefore, during my teenage years, I fought the idea of doing what my mother and father did. However, I learned that the apple doesn't fall far from the tree, and the examples I had with my parents played a more significant influence in my life that I would later appreciate.

At sixteen, I moved from Venezuela to the United States with $500 in my hands, leaving behind a country at the beginning of turmoil and speaking very little English. Though filled with sacrifices, this journey was a quest for safety and prosperity. I faced the challenges of adapting to a new culture, language, and educational system, finding comfort and guidance in the homes of relatives and friends.

I was inspired to pursue a career in nursing and healthcare, a journey inspired by my mother's dedication as our community nurse in our Venezuelan town while also being an entrepreneur. Observing her care for others and leading the family business with my dad sparked my desire to emulate her path, even though I barely understood her work as a child. I observed how, together with my dad, they built a profitable, successful business. It was a great example of teamwork and women's empowerment.

In the U.S., my uncle played a crucial role in my adaptation, guiding me through the intricacies of the American education system. This support led me to achieve an associate's degree in nursing, a stepping stone towards my goal of becoming a nurse scientist. During my early professional journey as a nurse, my sister was diagnosed with Neuromyelitis Optica (NMO), adding complexity to my adaptation to the U.S. This influenced my decision to pursue advanced degrees in nursing, fostering a sense of duty and compassion in me.

I began my career, like many immigrants, by attending a community college because it was affordable. Hostos Community College in the Bronx, NYC, became my home and where I discovered a new "familia". Nursing school was challenging but totally worth it. Looking back, I would not change my path at all, and I am extremely proud of my early beginnings at community college. After completing my associate's and immediately my bachelor's degree in nursing, my thirst for knowledge felt unquenched. A friend's suggestion led me to explore Pace University and the Lienhard School of Nursing. I was drawn to a unique nurse practitioner program offering a cadaver dissection course, which satiated my fascination with biology and confirmed that I was in the right place for me.

When I started my studies at Pace, my vision was clear: to become a Nurse Practitioner. The thought of engaging in research immediately after graduation was not on my radar. Yet, my academic and professional journey took a remarkable turn as I was encouraged by my mentors to continue and pursue a doctoral degree. This decision would make me the first in my family to earn a Ph.D. I received my Ph.D. in Nursing from the University of Pennsylvania. Their mentorship was invaluable, laying the foundation for my professional path.

My studies in Genomics and the Chemical Senses, a path less traveled in nursing, were influenced by my coursework at Pace and a curiosity about the human body that steered me toward basic science. Unplanned by me, but again influenced by mentors after my Ph.D., I went on to do a postdoctoral fellowship at the National Institute of Health (NIH). Later, I joined the faculty as a non-tenured Assistant Clinical Investigator, then joined the tenure track path, becoming the second nurse in the Country to receive the Lasker Clinical Research Scholar Award at the NIH and NIH Distinguished Scholar. Now, I am the Chief of the Sensory Science and Metabolism Laboratory at the National Institute on Alcohol Abuse and Alcoholism and co-director of the National Taste and Smell Center.

During the Coronavirus disease 2019 (COVID-19) pandemic, my expertise in chemosensory disorders became particularly relevant, allowing me to contribute to understanding how the virus impacted the senses of taste and smell for many around the globe. This led me to co-found the Global Consortium for Chemosensory Research. At the pandemic's peak, we conducted a large collaborative worldwide scientific study to assess the possible relationships between respiratory illness (e.g., COVID-19, influenza, or the common cold) and their effects on smell and taste. This work, which I do in my laboratory, along with my global health efforts through the Amazing Grace Children's Charity in Ghana, underscores my belief in the profound impact of nursing on community and global health.

Throughout my career, the significance of mentorship has been evident from the start. Mentors opened the doors to research for me, providing my first hands-on experience with scholarly work. My involvement in the Jonas Project and contributions to the book "Nursing Leadership: A Concise Encyclopedia" were milestones in my academic journey, offering early exposure to nurse scientists and the importance of seizing every opportunity, such as grants and scholarships, for professional growth. Now, I get to pay it forward by mentoring students and seeing them achieve their goals, which is among the most fulfilling aspects of my career. I advocate for the importance of mentorship, curiosity, and the pursuit of knowledge. Sharing my journey,

I aim to guide future healthcare leaders, emphasizing that the path to success is neither straight nor perfect but requires hard work and dedication.

My journey into clinical research underscores the potential nurses have to drive change by developing new knowledge. As a nurse scientist, being at the forefront of discovery has been both a privilege and a responsibility. I advise nurses internationally considering this Ph.D. path to remain open-minded, embrace the journey with perseverance, and be ready for the unexpected. The universe has a way of aligning opportunities that can lead to remarkable outcomes far beyond initial expectations. In nursing, I discovered a niche that allows me to be myself without compromising my passion for science and my desire to help people in need. As a nurse scientist, I can conduct research that improves the field of nursing and health outcomes.

As I reflect on my journey from being a young girl inspired by her mother's compassion to being a nurse and nurse scientist recognized for my contributions to nursing science and global health, advocacy has also been key to my journey. Witnessing healthcare inequities in my community from a young age, I was firmly determined to create tangible change. Nursing allowed me to do just that. Nursing is not only a remarkable career to serve and care for others, but as nurses, we hold a unique position of influence and trust, serving not only as caregivers but as powerful advocates for our patients and communities. My role as a nurse compels me to speak out against inequalities, challenge injustices, and work tirelessly to ensure that everyone receives the compassion, respect, and quality care they deserve, regardless of their background, identity, or socioeconomic status.

Looking at my journey into nursing, research, and healthcare advocacy, it's evident that my path was about providing care and confronting and challenging systemic injustices that lead to health disparities. This commitment led me to a career where I could address these issues head-on and advocate for those whose voices are often silenced.

My cultural heritage, a blend of Venezuelan vibrancy and Haitian strength, has influenced my approach to life and work. Being multicultural has been a great source of inspiration for innovative thinking, a holistic view of problems, and a solid commitment to meaningful work. This unique perspective is evident in my research by giving me a unique lens through which I view and investigate taste, smell, and emotions, as well as my advocacy and philanthropic work to improve health and well-being.

Throughout my career, I have sought to embody the principles of resilience and advocacy, taking on leadership roles, speaking out against injustices, and mentoring the next generation of healthcare professionals. My journey, marked by the obstacles I've overcome and the systemic issues I continue to fight against, is a testament to an individual's impact. Inspired by the collective outcry following George Floyd's death, my work is dedicated to ensuring that in healthcare, we address not just the physical needs of our patients but also the social determinants that impact their health and well-being.

As someone who has faced discrimination, ageism, and deep-seated inequities within our healthcare system, I have remained committed to the vision of a more equitable and just healthcare system. My story, intertwined with the broader social justice narrative, underscores the need for continuous advocacy and action to dismantle the barriers preventing many from accessing the care and opportunities they deserve. It's a reminder that the fight for health equity is inextricably linked to the fight for racial and social justice, and it's a fight that requires the commitment and courage of us all.

As a researcher and an underrepresented minority in research myself, I have a keen awareness of the importance of representation in research of underrepresented communities because research that includes perspectives from diverse cultural backgrounds can better address specific health needs and wellness practices that may be prevalent or unique to those in our communities which is critical for more inclusive and effective health interventions. I have learned that by incorporating underrepresented perspectives, research can redefine what is considered 'normal' or 'standard' in health and well-being. This redefinition can lead to a broader understanding of human experiences and conditions, leading to innovative research methodologies or new approaches to health and wellness that consider cultural and emotional aspects alongside physical symptoms.

Furthermore, as an Afro-Latina Scientist, leading and participating in research helps inspire others from our communities to engage in scientific fields, promoting diversity in these areas. I advise aspiring nurses and scientists to embrace their identity, face challenges boldly, and let their unique perspectives guide them. Seek mentors, build a supportive community, and never underestimate the power of dreams.

My journey is marked by growth, learning, and a deeper understanding of myself and the world. Being an agent of change involves adaptation, learning, and sharing wisdom. My story, rooted in Venezuela and Haiti, showcases resilience and the power of aligning passion with purpose. As I continue my work, I aim to inspire and empower others in science and exploration, fostering inclusivity and innovation. My narrative is a testament to the significance of heritage, the value of community, and the potential that arises from dreaming big and persevering through challenges. I share my journey to ignite a spirit of discovery and innovation in others, emphasizing the worth of their unique experiences and perspectives.

THE LEARNINGS

The journey to where I stand today, as a leader and innovator in my field, has been lined with a series of significant challenges, each demanding its own set of strategies and inner resources. Reflecting on these hurdles, I recognize their pivotal role in sculpting the resilient and driven individual I have become.

One of the most formidable challenges was the cultural and emotional transition from Venezuela to the United States at a young age. This transition was one of my earliest challenges, embedding a deep sense of resilience within me. The feeling of isolation and the pressure to adapt to a new language and culture was overwhelming. I overcame this by embracing my cultural identity and turning it into a source of strength and uniqueness rather than a barrier. Though from afar, my family's and community's support reminded me of home and identity. My perseverance was fortified by the support of relatives and friends of my family, who provided a sense of community and belonging in a foreign land.

Another significant challenge was navigating the competitive and often exclusive world of Science, Technology, Engineering, and Mathematics (STEM) as a Latina immigrant. The road was rife with biases and stereotypes, which sometimes made me question my place and potential. I found inner strength by focusing on my capabilities and contributions rather than the perceptions of others. I surrounded myself with mentors and peers who supported and believed in me, and their encouragement was crucial in building my confidence and resilience. Networking within professional communities also provided a platform to share experiences and strategies, reinforcing my determination to succeed. Engaging in professional communities, I found strength in shared experiences and strategies, reinforcing my determination to succeed against the odds.

One of the most valuable lessons I learned was to view failures and mistakes not as setbacks but as stepping stones. There were moments when things didn't go as planned, and projects or goals seemed to falter. Each mistake became a lesson in humility and adaptability, teaching me the importance of persistence and innovative thinking. As I faced these challenges, my goals and dreams evolved. I learned to redefine success, embrace the journey with all its detours, and continually adapt my aspirations to the lessons learned. This adaptability has been crucial in maintaining focus and direction, even when the path ahead seemed uncertain.

In my professional journey, I learned to challenge established norms and advocated for diversity and representation in science and healthcare. Despite my qualifications and evident passion, there were instances where my aspirations, especially in research and leadership, were deemed too ambitious for my age. The challenges of discrimination and ageism I faced along the way only fueled my determination to make a difference, to ensure that the healthcare system becomes a place where everyone can "breathe" freely, receiving the care and respect they deserve.

It was against this backdrop of personal and systemic challenges that the tragic death of George Floyd and his haunting last words, "I can't breathe," resonated deeply with me. This moment in history underscored the urgent need for systemic change—not just in law enforcement but within all structures of society, including healthcare. Floyd's plea became a rallying cry for me and many others, a stark reminder of the work that still needs to be done to dismantle systems of oppression that suffocate marginalized communities. Armed with this renewed sense of urgency, I sought opportunities that would help me gain more experience in health policy. I was nominated and became the Inaugural American Academy of Nursing Fellow at the National Academy of Medicine.

With this in mind, I actively participate in initiatives supporting underrepresented STEM groups, sharing my story and insights to inspire change. These efforts were not without resistance, but I persevered, driven by the conviction that a diverse scientific community is crucial for comprehensive and innovative research. These experiences taught me the importance of adaptability, persistence, and self-belief.

I realized the value of a supportive community and the impact of mentorship. As an Afro-Caribbean Latina born and raised in Venezuela of Haitian parents, I understood the importance of supporting opportunities for people of Latino heritage in nursing and nursing-related fields. While working toward my Ph.D. at Penn Nursing in 2013, I co-founded the Latino Nurses Network[1] now a 501c3 non-profit organization created to support the development and vision of current and future Latino nurse leaders, advocates, researchers, educators, and clinicians who are working to improve the health of their communities at the local, national and international level. I looked around the school and noticed so many predoctoral students and postdoctoral fellows who were Latino. I wanted to convene a group to share our successes and challenges. Together with another colleague who was a postdoctoral fellow, we gathered a group for dinner, and the Latino Nurses Network was created.

---

(1) https://www.latinonursesnetwork.org/

We turned to our community and leveraged our National Association of Hispanic Nurses[2] membership to make this vibrant, supportive network happen. What started as a small group has grown into a strong support network with over 1,000 members across different platforms. I advise those embarking on similar paths to embrace your unique journey, leverage your cultural strengths, and not shy away from challenges. Build a support system, seek mentorship, and remember that every challenge is an opportunity for growth. Keep moving forward, fueled by the knowledge that your journey, with all its struggles and triumphs, is paving the way for a more prosperous, diverse future.

THE INSPIRATION

Throughout my journey, inspiration has come from many sources, each shaping my path and fortifying my resolve during challenging times. Initially, my foremost inspiration was my family's resilience and dedication. My parents' sacrifices and foresight in seeking a better future for me in the United States instilled a deep sense of responsibility and ambition within me. Their stories and the cultural tapestry of Venezuela and Haiti provided a rich backdrop of inspiration, driving me to honor their sacrifices through my achievements.

I found role models in educators and mentors who embodied the values of resilience, innovation, and leadership. They showed me that tenacity and courage could transform barriers into stepping stones. Significant books and narratives of other scientists and leaders who had overcome adversity also became beacons of motivation. Learning about their journeys instilled a belief in the power of perseverance and the impact one individual can make. These stories were not just tales of success but testimonies of the relentless pursuit of dreams amidst obstacles.

---

(2) https://www.nahnnet.org/

My mother, a nurse, has been a continuous source of inspiration. Her dedication to caring for others and her compassion in her work laid the foundation for my path in health and science. Seeing her impact on patients' lives ignited my passion for healthcare and research. Similarly, my father, a professor, was a monumental figure in shaping my intellectual curiosity. He dedicated countless hours to supplement our education, often saying, "Your inheritance is your education. Your education will be the passport to see the world with new eyes and visit places you never imagined." His words rang true, as science has taken me to beautiful places, allowing me to explore, discover, and contribute globally. My parents often shared stories of their struggles and triumphs in Haiti, illustrating their profound impact on shaping my values and aspirations.

My parents were born in Haiti and grew up during the Duvalier Regime- this was an autocratic hereditary dictatorship in Haiti that lasted almost 29 years from 1957 until 1986. In 1980, my dad moved to Venezuela and later returned to marry my mother, who would join him in Caracas. Later in their life, they would become Venezuelan Citizens and now American Citizens. My sister and I were born and raised in Guatire, Venezuela, and later immigrated to the United States of America. Growing up, there were many stories shared in our household. One particular memory that stands out is when both my father and mother, against all odds, secured a scholarship for their education, demonstrating the power of perseverance and hard work. My mom received a scholarship from a German priest to attend nursing school. She became a nurse and supported her entire family with the stipend she was paid during school and later. Later, in Venezuela, she did not practice as a nurse much but was the go-to person in our community for health-related questions.

My father received a Jesuit scholarship and went on to become a teacher. Both used to study at times with kerosene lamps or under the street lamps to compensate for the nights in which the country was experiencing an energy crisis. This story always reminds me of the importance of dedication, innovation, and education and has been a guiding light in my life. Of course, like many immigrants to a new country, my parents had to make practical decisions; my father took all his skills, became an entrepreneur, and taught my sister and me financial literacy and entrepreneurship from an early age. With his pedagogical skills, he became our private tutor and taught us English, Math, and Physics at home, which allowed us to be ahead in school. Word got out in our community, and he developed a tutoring program where we would later have an opportunity to contribute and work.

My shared cultures have also been a source of continual inspiration. The Haitian Revolution, led by figures like Toussaint Louverture and El Libertador Simon Bolivar, has always motivated me. These stories of resilience and celebrating heritage instill a deep sense of pride and responsibility, encouraging me to incorporate these values into my professional and personal life. This rich cultural background has infused me with a sense of purpose and a unique perspective that I bring to my work and interactions. The resilience and perseverance of my parents and women in science like Marie Curie, the renowned physicist and chemist overcoming numerous societal barriers, provide a concrete example that has guided me. Despite facing gender discrimination and financial challenges, she made groundbreaking discoveries, inspiring me to push through obstacles in my career.

In my professional journey, witnessing the impact of my work on others has been incredibly motivating both as a nurse and a scientist. For example, seeing how my research in sensory science helped me understand why patients exhibited those symptoms during the COVID-19 pandemic was incredibly motivating. This breakthrough addressed a pressing health issue and brought a community closer together, emphasizing the real-world impact of scientific research, which led me to co-found the Global Consortium for Chemosensory Research, such as breakthroughs in research, influential collaborations, or significant recognitions. These milestones and pivotal points remind me why I embarked on this path. These moments remind me of the tangible difference my efforts make and fuel my commitment to continued innovation and service.

My vision for the future is one where science is inclusive and reflective of diverse perspectives, motivating me to break barriers and establish a more equitable scientific community. This vision drives me to mentor young scientists, especially those from underrepresented backgrounds, fostering a more diverse and innovative field.

THE ADVICE

Reflecting on my journey and the myriad of experiences that have shaped it, I realize there are invaluable pieces of advice I would impart to my younger self or anyone embarking on a similar path. These insights are born from the triumphs and the tribulations that have marked my way and are not just lessons but beacons to guide others not to be afraid of taking the road less traveled. I knew I was taking the road less traveled, but I have not walked it alone- I leaned on my community, and you can, too.

"Be fearless. Have the courage to take risks. Go where there are no guarantees. Get out of your comfort zone, even if it means being uncomfortable. The road less traveled is sometimes fraught with barricades, bumps, and uncharted terrain. But it is on that road where your character is truly tested. And have the courage to accept that you're not perfect, nothing is, and no one is — and that's OK." ~ Katie Couric

Embrace your unique story as it weaves the fabric of your experiences, cultural heritage, and individual journey that sets you apart and gives you a distinctive voice and perspective. Your background is not just a part of who you are; it can significantly drive your success and impact. This resonates with a quote by Roy T. Bennett "To shine your brightest light is to be who you truly are." Today I would tell my younger self to wear her heritage proudly and draw strength and inspiration from it, as it is an irreplaceable asset in life's journey. A lesson I learned from my mentors who encouraged me to bring my whole self into everything I did because I am who I am today for accepting my true identity -walk in your truth!

The importance of mentorship cannot be overstated, both seeking it and offering it. My mentors have been lighthouses throughout my career, guiding me through uncertain waters with their wisdom and experience. Similarly, becoming a mentor has allowed me to give back, share my journey, and learn through the fresh perspectives of those I guide. Mentorship is a beautiful, reciprocal relationship that enriches both the mentor and the mentee and is something I wish I had engaged in even more deeply and earlier. Reflecting on a time when I received an unexpected appreciation from a student for my mentorship profoundly shifted my perspective. This moment of gratitude made me realize the immense impact of small acts of kindness and guidance. It reminded me that our contributions, often unnoticed, can significantly influence others' lives. This realization grounded me in humility and opened my eyes to the value of every interaction, leading me to approach my work and relationships with greater empathy and mindfulness.

Resilience, the quiet strength that allows you to rise every time you fall, is critical. Life and careers are rarely linear or smooth. They are filled with setbacks and challenges that test your mettle. Embracing resilience means viewing these hurdles as opportunities for growth, learning from failure, and persevering with a renewed sense of purpose. Cultivating a resilient mindset from the outset would have prepared me even better for the twists and turns of my path.

Our journeys are ever-evolving, and so are we. Continuous learning and adaptability are crucial in a world that is constantly changing. Staying curious, open to new ideas, and flexible in the face of change are traits that I've found invaluable. They have allowed me to navigate new territories, embrace innovation, and remain relevant and impactful in my work.

In the relentless pursuit of goals and dreams, I've learned the importance of prioritizing self-care and well-being. It's easy to be consumed by ambitions and responsibilities, but neglecting your physical, mental, and emotional health can be detrimental in the long run. Establishing routines and habits that support a balanced life, finding time for rest and reflection, and nurturing your passions and relationships are essential for sustained success and happiness. Be conscious of your environmental footprint and make choices promoting sustainability and social good. Engage in practices and careers that benefit you and contribute positively to society and the environment, nurturing a legacy of responsibility and care for our planet and its inhabitants.

Lastly, building a supportive community has been instrumental. Surrounding yourself with people who uplift, understand, and challenge you creates a nurturing environment for personal and professional growth. These relationships provide comfort during tough times, joy in celebrations, and wisdom in decision-making. The community is a source of strength and a reminder that no journey is solitary. These pieces of advice, woven together, form a guiding philosophy I've come to live by. They are not just lessons learned but are the essence of a journey well-traveled, offering light and wisdom to those who follow. By sharing these insights, others may find the encouragement, understanding, and strength to navigate their paths with resilience, purpose, and joy.

A personal mantra that has been a constant inspiration throughout my journey is 'In the middle of difficulty lies opportunity" by Albert Einstein. This quote resonates deeply with me, reminding me that challenges are not just obstacles but gateways to growth and new possibilities. It has encouraged me to embrace difficulties positively, seeking hidden opportunities in every situation.

THE PATH FORWARD

Although my journey is unique to me, it encompasses themes that touch us all. My goal is to inspire you to embrace yourself as you appreciate the power of resilience and actively seek happiness and personal growth while understanding the significance of support and community. May you draw inspiration and courage from the lessons I have learned along the way.

Trust in the power of your dreams and the uniqueness of your voice. Never underestimate your capability to achieve extraordinary things. Embrace your heritage as a source of strength and inspiration, allowing it to guide your journey and enrich your perspective. Remember, success is not a solitary journey but one enriched by the support, wisdom, and collaboration of others. Together, our impact is amplified, and our successes are shared.We can go far by staying curious and adaptable. The world is ever-changing, and continuous learning is key to navigating and shaping it. Embrace new experiences and challenges as opportunities to grow and expand your horizons.

I encourage you to be a vocal advocate for fair treatment, opportunities, and resources. In both personal and professional realms, it's crucial to stand up for yourself, negotiate for what you deserve, and remain steadfast in your values and rights. Advocating for oneself is about asserting your position and ensuring fairness and respect in all interactions. Recognize and celebrate the vast diversity among Latinas. Support and uplift one another, understanding that our varied backgrounds and experiences are sources of strength and inspiration.

Another mantra that has guided me is 'Be the change you wish to see in the world' by Mahatma Gandhi. It reminds me that each of us has the power to make a difference, starting with our actions and decisions, and that power lies within us. Let this be our shared call to action, a commitment to live with purpose, passion, and persistence.

As a Latina scientist, I represent a breakthrough in the male-dominated field of STEM that has been predominantly homogeneous culturally. I hope to encourage women and minorities by showcasing how diversity within science enriches research efforts. This leads to perspectives and groundbreaking discoveries.

I'd love for my story to be a catalyst for your journey. Approach the future with courage, love, and an indomitable spirit. The path may not always be easy, but it is yours to shape and illuminate. Go forth with the knowledge that you are powerful, capable, and never alone. Rise together, for in unity lies our greatest strength and brightest future. Your story is as unique as mine, and it holds value. Pay it forward by sharing it with others, allowing it to inspire those around us as we collectively strive to make an impact in our world.

ABOUT PAULE

Paule V. Joseph, Ph.D., MBA, MS, FNP-BC, FTCNS, FAAN, is a renowned Venezuelan-Haitian-American nurse scientist and clinician who has markedly impacted chemosensory (taste and smell) science, genomics, and precision health. She serves as a Lasker Clinical Scholar at the National Institutes of Health (NIH) and a Distinguished Scholar at the National Institute on Alcohol Abuse and Alcoholism (NIAAA) and the National Institute of Nursing Research (NINR). She is Chief of the Sensory Science and Metabolism Section (SenSMet) at the Division of Intramural Clinical and Biological Research and co-director of the NIH National Taste and Smell Center. A testament to her diverse skill set, Dr. Joseph's educational background encompasses both nursing and the biological sciences. She received an AAS in Nursing at Hostos Community College, a BSN from the College of New Rochelle, a Master of Science with a specialty as a Family Nurse Practitioner from Pace University, and an Executive MBA from Quantic School of Business and Technology.

She completed her Ph.D. at the University of Pennsylvania. She conducted her Ph.D. work at the Monell Chemical Senses Center (the only center in the world dedicated to training on taste & smell), where she focused on sensory biology and genomics. She then completed a Clinical and Translational Postdoctoral Fellowship at the NINR supported by the Office of Workforce Diversity. With over 100 publications, she is a recognized figure in sensory science research. Her work has been showcased in top-tier academic journals and captured the attention of the media, such as TIME, NPR, and the New York Times. She is particularly interested in understanding how sensory function and dysfunction influence well-being and health outcomes, especially in populations disproportionately affected by health disparities. Her insights have been highlighted in various media outlets, reflecting her role as a leading voice in her field. Her research explores how taste and smell influence health & well-being, especially in those with chronic illnesses. Specifically, she investigates the neurological mechanisms of chemosensation and its relation to ingestive behaviors, especially in those with obesity and substance use disorders. Notably, during the COVID-19 pandemic, she examined the effects of the virus on taste and smell and co-founded the Global Consortium for Chemosensory Research[1] Dr. Joseph is a devoted advocate for diversity in science.

She mentors and fosters inclusivity, especially for underrepresented individuals and women in science. She also leads initiatives such as the Amazing Grace Children's Charity[2] in Ghana, where she is the Director of Medical Services President of the African Research Academy for Women[3] and Vice-President of the Latino Nurses Network[4]. Dr. Joseph has been honored with multiple awards from several global organizations such as the Friends of the National Institutes of Nursing Research, the National Minority Quality Forum, the National Association of Hispanic Nurses, the Johnson & Johnson- American Association of Colleges of Nursing, and The Rockefeller University Heilbrunn Nurse Scholar. She has been recognized with the Ajinomoto Award for Young Investigators in Gustation from the Association of Chemoreception Sciences. She is a fellow of the American Academy of Nursing, a Fellow of the New York Academy of Medicine, a Fellow of the Transcultural Nursing Society, and a member of the Royal Society of Medicine, United Kingdom. She is also the Inaugural American Academy of Nursing Fellow at the National Academy of Medicine in the United States of America. Dr. Joseph's commitment to advancing awareness, research, and health of the Chemical Senses and her exceptional skill in integrating complex scientific concepts into clinical practice, public awareness, and policy have made her a valuable contributor to sharing insights on the intersection of sensory experiences (smell) and overall well-being. She practices clinically as a certified nurse practitioner working at the NIH.

---

(1) https://gcchemosensr.org/
(2) https://agccharity.org/
(3) https://www.africanwomenresearchers.org/
(4) https://www.latinonursesnetwork.org/

Learn more and connect with Paule at:
NIH https://irp.nih.gov/pi/paule-joseph
LinkedIn https://www.linkedin.com/in/paulevjoseph
X https://twitter.com/Dr_Paulevj
Instagram https://www.instagram.com/dr_paulejoseph/?hl=en
Threads https://www.threads.net/@dr_paulejoseph
Wikipedia https://en.wikipedia.org/wiki/Paule_Valery_Joseph

DISCLAIMER:
The content is solely the responsibility of the author and does not necessarily represent the official views of the National Institutes of Health and/or Health and Human Services.

SONIA ENDLER

"You can dare to dream big regardless of your circumstances!"

- Sonia Endler

~ ~ ~

Sonia is a highly accomplished senior financial executive with over two decades of experience providing strategic financial governance, driving financial growth, and optimizing operational efficiency. Throughout her extensive career, she has served as a trusted advisor to iconic media and entertainment corporations, including MGM Studios, Tribune Media, FOX, E! Networks, and Paramount Pictures, crafting strategies that not only enhance top-and-bottom performance but also maximize return on investment, leading to transformative successes. Currently, she serves as the CEO of Galactic Road, LLC, a private investment company specializing in real estate and diverse business ventures.

~ ~ ~

A la mujer que me formó, mi primera maestra, y la que me mostró la esencia de ser una mujer con sueños, valentía y espíritu emprendedor,

Mamá, eres mi primera y eterna fuente de inspiración. Tu capacidad para superar las dificultades, tu espíritu emprendedor para realizar tus sueños y continuar creciendo a lo largo de la vida han sido mi fuente de fortaleza. Tu amor, sabiduría y espíritu continúan moldeando mi camino, y dedico estas páginas a ti con inmenso agradecimiento y amor.

Con toda mi admiración, tu hija que te adora,
Sonia

FROM LIMA TO LOS ANGELES, A LEGACY OF GROWTH AND RESILIENCE

THE JOURNEY

I was born and raised in Lima, Peru, attending an all-girls Catholic school from kindergarten to 9th grade. Throughout that time, I was fortunate to be surrounded by a warm and supportive community of friends and teachers, shaping me into a dedicated student who craved learning and yearned for new experiences.

My parents, especially my mother, envisioned a brighter future where possibilities were endless for my sisters and me, a future where we could reach our full potential. At 14, a pivotal moment occurred in my life as I transitioned from Lima to Los Angeles, joining my 17-year-old sister to start a new life in the United States while my parents stayed behind, providing support from home.

I arrived first in Orlando, Florida, with my mother and grandmother, and we had a fantastic time exploring several amusement parks and creating cherished memories. I am grateful for my mom's clever idea to take me to the amusement parks first because I was enthusiastic and instantly fell in love with the U.S. This experience helped me make a smooth transition to a country I had never been to. Approximately one week later, we reunited with my sister in Los Angeles and spent several weeks together. After that, my mother and grandmother returned home, leaving my sister and me to pursue better education and opportunities.

Despite missing my family and friends back home, I wholeheartedly embraced the change, fueled by the excitement of countless opportunities awaiting me. I began my educational journey in the U.S., attending the local public high school, which marked a complete adjustment from my previous school experience. It was larger, co-ed, and resembled the college life I had envisioned back home. In this new environment, I saw elements like letterman jackets, lockers, and cheerleaders that we didn't have in my school back home, but were reminiscent of one of my favorite American TV shows that I used to watch in Peru called 'Happy Days.' While these may seem trivial, they gave me a sense of familiarity and excitement about being in a completely different environment.

I was placed in English as a Second Language (ESL) classes and instantly made friends with shared experiences as immigrants, creating a strong bond among us. I loved adventure and learning new things; the concept of electives and the ability to co-create my academic curriculum were new to me. Back home, every student graduated high school with the same curriculum. I cherished the freedom and responsibility to choose some of my courses. I eagerly immersed myself in this exciting environment with many wonderful options.

I signed up for numerous extracurricular activities, including sports teams such as Track & Field, Soccer, and Volleyball. Balancing high school commitments while working part-time kept me engaged and focused, culminating in graduating in the top 3% of my class.

My journey continued as I pursued a degree in Business Administration with an emphasis in Finance from the University of Southern California. Among many interests, I chose finance as my career path, driven by my desire to acquire new skills that could maximize my chances of success. I was eager for my parents to see one day that their monumental sacrifice was worthwhile; this intention became a guiding force. Their selflessness inspired me to be resourceful, seek opportunities, and strive to reach my full potential.

USC opened the door to a world of new possibilities, not just in terms of education but also through the community of outstanding individuals who surrounded me. Their brilliance and ambitious goals inspired me to dream bigger. The most wonderful gift was making lifelong friends who are still part of my inner circle, and their influence continues to shape me today.

I began my finance career in the media and entertainment industry, feeling incredibly fortunate to land my first job as a financial analyst at an iconic Hollywood studio. Despite intense competition in this industry and having no connections, I believe my enthusiasm and dedication shone through during the interview process, ultimately enabling me to secure the position. I was filled with excitement and gratitude, making it my mission to meet and exceed expectations. It wasn't just about a paycheck, but about establishing a stellar reputation and making significant contributions to my organization.

In the early years of my career, there were only a few Latinos in the office, and I deeply appreciated the opportunity to contribute to such a fun and dynamic industry. Working in international divisions during this period, the overall environment's openness to diverse cultures and backgrounds made me feel at home. Additionally, I was surrounded by brilliant women in mid-level positions who served as incredible role models. Excelling at my job became a source of great pride for me, and I aimed to consistently deliver outstanding results. I developed an approach to observing my peers in positions one level above mine so that I could be prepared and selected when opportunities arose. This approach proved successful, leading to my promotion to Director of Finance at the age of 26, and a few years later to Vice President.

Fast forward to today, I am incredibly grateful for the privilege of dedicating over 20 years to the media & entertainment industry, serving in various finance roles, including the position of CFO, within iconic companies such as MGM, Tribune Media, FOX, E! Networks, and Paramount Pictures, among others. I am genuinely passionate about my commitment to empowering aspiring leaders, particularly Latinas. Currently, I serve as a board member of non-profit organizations that focus on supporting the next generation of women and Latino leaders. I hope my journey is a testament to daring to chase your dreams regardless of circumstances and underscores the power of determination, resilience, and a supportive community to achieve one's dreams and pay it forward.

THE LEARNINGS

I realized that my promotion to Vice President of Finance represented not only a significant opportunity, but also a great display of confidence in my abilities. Consequently, I was ready to show I could thrive in this new role. Often, I was the youngest, the only woman, and the only Latina in a male-dominated finance world, especially in sports.

As a young executive, I was finding my footing, but the notable absence of women, especially women of color, as role models and mentors presented a distinct challenge. In an effort to integrate, I observed the prevailing culture. I often took cues from the leadership styles of successful male peers, hoping this approach could guide me in the right direction. However, I quickly realized that what worked for men didn't always work for women. For example, most male leaders were tough and distant, which created an aura of unapproachability. I started wondering if my naturally engaging and warm disposition aligned well with the expectations of this professional setting.

Being the adaptable person that I am, I tried adopting a stern demeanor. However, I quickly recognized that it did not work. My conversations lacked the level of engagement and openness that I had experienced in the past. I recognized that it was crucial for me to strike the right balance between friendliness and assertiveness, but my male colleagues did not seem to face the same concerns. While I was able to achieve positive results, it was hard to fit into an environment where I experienced heightened self-awareness in my interactions and couldn't truly be myself. This experience taught me valuable lessons in balancing adaptability while ensuring that my values align with the workplace culture.

What sustained me through these challenging times was a deep sense of gratitude for each opportunity to learn and make a meaningful impact. When our company underwent a reorganization, it marked a significant turning point. We found ourselves part of a new team, blending not only men and women, but women of color in finance leadership roles. These women leaders demonstrated that achieving success in leadership while staying true to oneself wasn't just a possibility; it was actively encouraged. Consequently, I took proactive steps to connect with more women executives within my organization whom I greatly admired. This involved seeking collaborative project opportunities or simply inviting them to casual lunches. I also made intentional efforts to connect with women leaders outside of the organization via LinkedIn, which sometimes meant requesting meetings or just following their journeys for inspiration. Witnessing the willingness of many women to support each other was truly wonderful. My network expanded further through engaging with professional communities dedicated to empowering women. Through these experiences, I realized that our well-being and success are closely tied to the culture in which we thrive.

As I recognized the importance of embracing my authentic self, it became more than just a personal journey; it turned into a mission. I hope to empower the next generation of female leaders, encouraging them to truly know themselves, bring their authentic selves to work, and pursue their paths to success. Being intentional about aligning with work cultures that resonate with my values has been an incredible journey of self-discovery and self-empowerment. It has shown me that I possess the ability to shape my professional environment, ensuring it not only nurtures and supports my growth but also provides me with the courage to be an agent of positive change. I hope my journey serves as inspiration for other women to embark on a similar path of self-awareness, self-love, and authenticity. In embracing our authentic selves, we empower not only ourselves but also pave the way for a more inclusive and diverse workplace for the next generation.

THE INSPIRATION

My career journey started with a huge dose of inspiration: my parents' sacrifice, separating from us while we were only teenagers so that we could have a chance at a better life in the United States. Their extraordinary courage fueled my determination to make their sacrifice truly count. I set my sights on reaching my full potential for myself and becoming a positive force for my family, community, and the world.

As life unfolded and I began my own family, my motivation took a beautiful turn. Now, my two children are the heartbeat of everything I do. I don't just want to be a parent; I aim to be a living example, showing them life's incredible possibilities. If I can overcome my obstacles, just imagine the amazing things they can achieve. I want to inspire them to dream big, reach for the stars, and strike a balance between a fulfilling career and family life. I want them to know they have the power to impact the world positively. In tough times, my children are my rock, guiding me toward choices that showcase courage, resilience, and self-respect so they can tap into their own superpowers when facing challenges.

Another wonderful source of inspiration comes from the people in my communities. Their ambitious goals and unwavering passion are a constant source of inspiration. The stories and achievements, especially from Latinos with similar backgrounds, inspire me to keep pushing boundaries, always looking for new ways to grow and contribute positively to the world.

I also enjoy watching inspirational movies, especially those based on true stories that defy all odds. Recently, I watched the movie 'A Million Miles Away'; it's an incredible story of perseverance, passion, and big dreams. What resonates most is that it's a Latino immigrant story, a reminder of the triumphs over challenges that parallel the experiences of many in the Latino community.

THE ADVICE

As I reflect on my journey, I would like to share advice that I hope will guide you on your own path to achieving your dreams.

Build Your Village; Community is Crucial:

Throughout your career journey, establishing a supportive community will play a critical role in your success. Don't wait for challenges to knock on your door—proactively seek out positive and encouraging individuals to include in your inner circle. Remember, you're not in this alone; a well-rounded community can play various roles, from friends and experts to sponsors and mentors. Tap into resources like Employee Resource Groups (ERGs), consider joining professional women's networking groups, or explore opportunities within your college alumni network. These relationships will not only uplift and inspire you but also provide the courage to take on new, bigger challenges. Additionally, remember to uplift other women along the way.

You are Your Top Investment:

Recognize your worth; treat yourself as the valuable investment you are. The time and resources you dedicate to your personal development will pay off in the long run. Do not shy away from confronting any uncertainties or apprehensions that may arise on your journey. Instead, tackle them head-on with a proactive approach. Whether it involves refining your networking skills, honing your public speaking abilities, pursuing advanced education, prioritizing your health and wellness, or seeking guidance through coaching, embrace each opportunity to enhance your personal development. This contributes to a more empowered, capable, and resilient version of yourself.

The Transformative Power of Self-Awareness and Self-Discovery:

In our fast-paced and dynamic world, the journey of self-awareness and self-discovery is a crucial aspect of personal development. This process empowers you to identify your strengths, weaknesses, passions, and values, ultimately guiding you toward environments where you can thrive. Understanding who you truly are lays the foundation for a more fulfilling and intentional life. Embracing self-awareness allows us to cultivate authenticity. Remember, the most fulfilling and meaningful life is one that reflects the essence of your true self.

Bring Your Authentic Self to Work and Choose Aligned Cultures:

Embrace your uniqueness, your Latinidad, and seek work environments that resonate with your values. Your well-being and success are deeply connected to the culture in which you thrive, so be intentional about choosing workplaces where you feel supported, valued, and where your authentic self can thrive.

Prioritize workplaces that not only recognize but also celebrate diversity and individuality. By doing so, you can cultivate a work environment that not only allows for personal growth but fosters a supportive environment and, in turn, contributes to a more inclusive and diverse professional community.

Pay Yourself First and Build an Emergency Fund Early in Your Career for Financial Stability:

It isn't just about the paycheck; it's about the freedom to operate from a position of strength. Shifting your mindset to focus on thriving rather than merely surviving will empower you to deliver your best work genuinely. If your workplace no longer aligns with your professional goals, you'll have the peace of mind that your financial foundation is solid. It's not just about having a job; it's about being able to make choices that serve you best. By paying yourself first, establishing a robust emergency fund, and initiating early investments, you set the stage for long-term financial well-being.

THE PATH FORWARD

I hope that by sharing my experiences and the lessons I've learned, I can inspire and empower other Latinas in their career journeys. Overcoming obstacles is possible through fostering a growth mindset and resilience, which can be achieved by engaging in personal development within a supportive community. It's essential to strike a balance between career aspirations and personal fulfillment.

I invite Latinas to discover their true selves, embrace authenticity, and seek workplace cultures aligned with their values. By actively contributing to the growth of inclusive and diverse professional environments, we can increase the visibility of Latina role models. By paving the way for the next generation of Latinas, we enable them to confidently pursue their dreams while staying true to themselves, making a lasting impact on the world.

ABOUT SONIA

Sonia is a highly accomplished senior financial executive with over two decades of experience in providing strategic financial governance, driving financial growth, and optimizing operational efficiency. Throughout her extensive career, she has served as a trusted advisor to iconic media and entertainment corporations, including MGM Studios, Tribune Media, FOX, E! Networks, and Paramount Pictures, crafting strategies that not only enhance top-and-bottom performance but also maximize return on investment, leading to transformative successes. Currently, she serves as the CEO of Galactic Road, LLC, a private investment company specializing in real estate and diverse business ventures.

During her tenure as the Executive Vice President of TV Finance at MGM Studios, Sonia played a pivotal role in overseeing significant growth and facilitating M&A support within her division, which culminated in the company's acquisition by Amazon for $8.5 billion. Prior to this, as the CFO of WGN America and Tribune Studios within Tribune Media, she was instrumental in the financial and operational transformation of two high-growth divisions, preparing them for acquisition. This ultimately led to the company being acquired by Nexstar for a value of $6.4 billion.

Sonia serves as a board member and audit committee member of Girl Scouts of Greater Los Angeles, and she is also an active board member for the University of Southern California's Latino Alumni Association. Additionally, she is an executive member of the Latino Corporate Directors Association (LCDA). Sonia holds a B.S. degree in business administration with an emphasis in Finance from the University of Southern California.

Born and raised in Lima, Peru, she currently resides in Los Angeles with her husband and two children.

Learn more and connect with Sonia at:
https://www.linkedin.com/in/soniaendler/

YAMILA CONSTANTINO

"Life's journey is anything but linear. It's a path strewn with rises and falls, with unexpected turns that somehow find their purpose and place in the grand tapestry of our lives'"

\- Yamila Constantino

~ ~ ~

Yamila Constantino Mendez is the accomplished founder and managing partner of eContent Digital, a leading content creation and digital marketing company connecting healthcare organizations with the Hispanic community. With over three decades of experience in media, including roles at Bloomberg, where she led production for multiple channels across languages and regions, Yamila is a multi-award-winning and Emmy-nominated media entrepreneur and former journalist.

~ ~ ~

For my mom, Patricia, my grandmothers Lupe and Ana, and my aunts Marta and Victoria, you have all been the sources of endless inspiration. For Felix, my partner in a life full of adventures, you have been the pillar of my strength. With heartfelt gratitude, I dedicate this chapter to you all.

TWISTS AND TURNS, EMBRACING LIFE'S UNEXPECTED JOURNEY

THE JOURNEY

The road is never a straight line.

My young self would be very surprised if she saw me today, proudly running my company that connects Hispanics with healthcare organizations through content and digital marketing.

I was born and raised in Mexico to a mother who worked as a homemaker and a father who was a lawyer. They didn't raise me as a traditional teenager. Instead of a quinceañera party, my parents sent me to a summer student exchange program in Wyoming to live with a family to improve my English. At 16 years old, I moved to Mexico City for university. Being so young, I really didn't know what I wanted to study, so at age 19, I dropped out. As much as my parents begged, I refused to stay one more year and graduate as a Graphic Designer.

This experience depressed me for a while. Eventually, I started taking acting classes. My passion for the theatre and the arts led me to relocate to New York, where I pursued my studies in acting at the Lee Strasberg Institute. After completing my courses, I intended to travel to Paris to audition for Peter Brook. The impact of his multilingual and multinational theatre group during their performance in Mexico had left a lasting impression on me.

While in New York, I thought I had found what I wanted to do for the rest of my life: be an actor.

But life has a funny way of changing your plans when you least expect it! I met my partner in life and ended up saying Au Revoir to my Paris plans! He came from Puerto Rico to finish his master's degree. He encouraged me to stay in New York and finish my college degree. I changed course and decided I would learn everything behind the camera. I was accepted at New York University and graduated with honors with a Communications and TV Production Bachelor of Arts.

News Reporting and Producing

After graduation, I began working as a reporter and producer for several TV shows on Spanish television networks. Eventually, I ended up at Bloomberg TV. Bloomberg was more of a startup when I joined. At the time, there wasn't even a human resources department. If you were entrepreneurial and had a good idea, Michael Bloomberg would let you run with it. I spent some of the most critical years of my professional life at Bloomberg.

There, I discovered my management skills. We were a small team, and since I do not like falling through the cracks and our boss didn't speak Spanish, I started managing our group, which consisted of four guys and myself. They called me the "queen bee" long before that moniker was applied to a certain famous singer. We launched the first personal finance report for national syndication on US Spanish radio stations and won the NY Press Award for best business writing. A colleague said, "But you report in Spanish!" I answered, "So what? Good writing is good writing, regardless of language!"

I was promoted to the Radio and TV Syndication manager position. My 40-person team produced 200 daily reports for over 900 affiliates in English and Spanish from Canada to Argentina. I also launched the first Spanish-language show for the Latin American channel, covering the economies and markets of all the Latin American countries.

My last position was in London as Head of Production for the five European channels in five languages: English, French, Italian, German, and Spanish. I was responsible for a 150-person team. This happened during the 2008 Financial Crisis that shook the world. It was intense. After two years in London, I decided to move on and left that job.

Little did I know that would be the beginning of my life as an entrepreneur.

Creating healthier Hispanic communities

While looking for a new job, I started helping my husband. He was a former media executive who mainly worked independently as a television and video producer and had several companies. He was hired to do a project with one of the largest hospitals in New York and asked me to executive-produce it. I also hosted the series. It was a health and wellness TV magazine. For a long time, I had been passionate about health and wellness, so I dove in. After almost a decade, we have grown our own company. I got certified as a Health Coach, and my mission has been to help US Hispanics take control of their health.

As you can see, the road is never a straight line, so you must be open to new learnings and opportunities. I could never have imagined the twists and turns my journey would take me on. You, too, will discover new skills and talents you didn't know you had. You must open your mind and embrace what life puts on the path for you.

THE LEARNINGS

Life has always been about learning new skills and having new experiences.

You don't have to be an expert to accept a new job or a promotion. When I joined Bloomberg TV and Radio, I was experienced in news reporting and production, not finance and economics. I nearly passed on the job, thinking that I wasn't a fit. However, once I got there, I found my broadcast and journalism background to be a unique asset among a sea of financial pros. Luckily, the company believed in training us. Before I knew it, I became a financial news reporter, hosting my show and digging into Latin American markets, interviewing the movers and shakers of the financial world.

The takeaway? Take advantage of opportunities, even if it's something you have never done before. Dive in, do your homework, and learn as you go. It also helps to have a go-to-friend when you are in uncharted territory. I had a friend who was a financial journalism veteran, and I wasn't shy about tapping her for insights when I needed them, especially at the beginning of this new chapter in my life.

Surround yourself with the best team and empower them.

My role is to be more of a coach than a boss with my team. Their wins reflect my leadership effectiveness, so I ensure they feel recognized, inspired, and fully engaged in our shared success. For me, personal and professional growth is a team sport- we all level up together. Without a strong team, a manager or an entrepreneur doesn't just stagnate, they miss out on the collective drive that propels a business forward.

Ultimately, the team is the company's heartbeat, capable of accelerating its success or stalling its progress. Your business can only succeed with a great team.

Embrace technology and AI.

Recently, two of our team members attended an international digital marketing conference in Amsterdam, where a key topic was the integration of Artificial Intelligence in content and digital marketing. The primary insight was that while AI won't supplant content creators and marketers, those who adeptly utilize AI will have a significant advantage over those who don't.

The ongoing debate about AI's potential risks to humanity is noteworthy. While hoping these concerns don't materialize, we recognize the importance of leveraging AI. In practice, we've been engaging with AI-driven tools for some time. This includes everyday utilities like autocomplete, grammar and spelling checkers, web translators, and editors. In video content, we've harnessed AI to upscale PDF images to 4K quality, a feat achievable with AI technology. So, while the debate continues, we must embrace technology to stay in the game.

Be bold and ask for help, especially when facing a life challenge.

Reach out for help when you're up against a significant life hurdle. I had a rough patch when I lost my dad —he was kidnapped, and they found him dead after a week of searching. It rocked me to my core. For months, I shut everyone out, just going through the motions of day-to-day life. Even during a workout, I'd find myself overwhelmed with tears.

It's easy to lash out at those closest to you when you're hurting. I was on edge, and my dear husband bore the brunt of my pain. Realizing I was spiraling, I started therapy. It was my lifeline, helping me heal without losing my marriage. Never feel embarrassed about admitting you need a hand, no matter the issue.

Always listen to your gut.

Trust your instincts. I've always relied on intuition rather than getting bogged down in overthinking. Often, my initial instincts guide me to the right outcome. I think about the times I've held back, not voicing my thoughts or doubting my ideas, only to watch someone else speak up or act on them. Pay attention to your gut feelings!

THE INSPIRATION

The roots of my inspiration stretch back to two remarkable women—my grandmothers. My paternal grandmother, a resilient soul, became a widow at 24. With little formal education and four children in her care, she channeled her entrepreneurial spirit, which first sparked at the tender age of 15 when she helped her widowed mother set up a food stall at the market. Her determination led her to own a restaurant and a small hotel, which she managed until she passed away at 94, having only recently retired from her restaurant business at 75. Her tenacity is a legacy I proudly carry on.

On the other side, my maternal grandmother was a whirlwind of activity, managing to run various home businesses while raising ten children. A blend of necessity and innate business acumen led her to open multiple businesses, including selling milk, cheese, and butter—a trade where I fondly recall assisting her. The memory of her unmatched cheese-making skills and the lost recipe is a cherished fragment of my heritage.

The influence of my grandmothers was strengthened by my aunts, who were pioneers in their way. In an era when women's roles were confined mainly to the home, they broke the mold as university-educated professionals; one became a psychiatrist, and the other a chemist, supporting their families and setting a precedent for me to follow.

My mother's journey is also a powerful inspiration: she began working out of the home after 50, despite not having a college degree. For a quarter of a century, she dedicated herself to a non-profit organization, building a successful career until retirement at 75. Now, at 82, her independence and financial security are sustained by the pension she earned through her years of steadfast work.

I can only aspire to become a beacon of inspiration for other women, just as my grandmothers, aunts, and mother have been for me, exemplifying unwavering resilience and strength.

Beyond family, books were a sanctuary, a window into the lives of trailblazing women who defied societal norms. I was captivated by the tales of George Sand, who donned men's clothing to access the literary clubs of Paris, and Isadora Duncan, the mother of Modern Dance.

And then there was the mythological figure of Ariadne, who played a crucial role in the defeat of the Minotaur and, despite Theseus's betrayal, found love with Dionysius, earning a place among the stars. Each story, real or mythic, woven with resilience and rebellion, helped shape the person I am today—a tapestry of entrepreneurial spirit, professional ambition, and the belief that every setback can lead to a new, star-studded path.

As a business owner, my inspiration is my former boss, Mike Bloomberg, and it has helped to shape my business ethos. His leadership was marked by generosity and a culture that genuinely celebrated merit, offering ample room for growth without the constraints of micromanagement. This approach instilled a sense of empowerment and accountability, driving me to prove my worth. When I took the reins in London, heading production for five European channels, I broke the mold of what was expected of an "American" leader. I bring this spirit of defying stereotypes and fostering an environment of trust and opportunity to my company, striving to uplift and empower my team just as I was.

THE ADVICE

Embrace emotional intelligence: The key to thriving in life and work.

For me, emotional intelligence is the unsung hero of a fulfilling life, offering the gift of deeper connections, profound self-awareness, and heartfelt empathy. It's about making wise, compassionate decisions and a vital element in carving a path to both personal and professional triumph.

Some people are born with it, but it can be acquired by increasing self-awareness, managing emotions effectively, and developing empathy -putting yourself in someone else's shoes. This can be achieved through mindfulness practices, active listening, and learning to understand and respond to others' emotions. Seeking feedback and being open to self-improvement are also crucial. It's a continuous growth process, enhancing personal and professional relationships.

Cultivate your entrepreneurial mindset.

My entrepreneurial streak has been part of me from the start. Looking back, it's evident that the seeds were there all along. In junior high, I joined forces with a few classmates to create a newsletter, discussing book reviews and the latest school buzz. When I was 14 or 15, I took the initiative to teach English to my cousins over the summer. Another year, I found myself guiding American tourists around town. This was all as a teenager!

If there's anything I would change, it would be to have realized that I had an entrepreneurial spirit and started my own company earlier instead of letting the fear of failure hold me back.

Exercise is not optional; it's really the best medicine.

I wish I'd realized sooner that working out isn't just a 'nice to have' habit—it's essential. It didn't click until my thirties when I noticed my arms weren't as firm as I wanted, so I got into it out of vanity. But once I got into the rhythm of regular workouts, there was no looking back. It's become my battery charger and my immune system booster. Even when I had an early start at work, I'd be up at five and hitting the gym by 5:30. Sure, people wondered how I managed to wake up that early. The secret? Don't overthink it—just like you don't debate whether to go to work or not, you don't debate that you must exercise regularly. Despite the early morning struggle, the buzz I got for the rest of the day made it a no-brainer.

And if you're wondering what fitness has to do with work or life experience, believe me, it's a game changer. It boosts you physically and prepares you mentally to tackle whatever life throws. Exercise is all about carving out time to cultivate your well-being. Exercise really is the best medicine.

Learn from your mistakes and get off your back.

Growing up, I took every slip-up hard, stewing over even the most minor blunders, chasing the ghost of Little Miss Perfect. It was a tough habit to shake, this dwelling on errors. But here's a little wisdom I've picked up: nobody's perfect. Messing up doesn't have to be a disaster. Own it, apologize if needed, make it right, and then let it go. Trust me, you'll handle it better next time. And sure, you'll trip up again—everyone does. It's just the way life rolls. So go easy on yourself. I've been down that road of self-criticism, and it's a dead end.

THE PATH FORWARD

Life's journey is anything but linear.

It's a path strewn with rises and falls, with unexpected turns that somehow find their purpose and place in the grand tapestry of our lives. Every step taken, every stumble, shapes you—each moment, whether wrapped in joy or shadowed by tribulation, holds its gift. So, relish the ride and embrace its unpredictability. When life hands you lemons, don't just make lemonade—create a masterpiece.

Reflecting on my path, it's been nothing short of astonishing. The young me never envisioned leading her company, making a home in vibrant New York or London, or traveling to see the world. Yet, here I am, and curiosity and gratitude have been my compass.

My aspiration? I want to forge a legacy that breathes life into healthier Hispanic communities, leveraging my expertise and zeal for wellness to uplift and transform. This is the dream I'm building, step by step, with the help of my team.

ABOUT YAMILA

Yamila Constantino Mendez is the accomplished founder and managing partner of eContent Digital, a leading content creation and digital marketing company connecting healthcare organizations with the Hispanic community. With over three decades of experience in media, including roles at Bloomberg, where she led production for multiple channels across languages and regions, Yamila is a multi-award-winning and Emmy-nominated media entrepreneur and former journalist.

Yamila is a New York University honor graduate, a two-time inclusion in Hispanic magazine's Top 100 Latinas list, and a winner of the US Hispanic Chamber of Commerce "At the Table Competition" for women entrepreneurs. She's won several Telly and Communicator awards.

She also leads the original content division at eContent TV. She is co-creator and executive producer of the Wine Outsiders series, soon to be launched on streaming platforms in multiple countries across the globe.

Yamila is also a certified Health Coach through the Dr. Sears Wellness Institute, an institution renowned for its science-based approach to supporting individuals to seize control of their health. She loves to exercise and has practiced yoga for two decades. Her other passion is traveling, and she hopes to visit as many countries as possible in her lifetime.

Learn more at:

www.econtentdigital.com

Surround yourself with Extraordinary Latinas who encourage you to thrive.

U+
UNITED LATINAS

ABOUT UNITED LATINAS

Empowering, Amplifying & Connecting Extraordinary Latina Leaders.

UNITED LATINAS is a collaborative organization devoted to empowering, amplifying, and connecting Latina Women to elevate their leadership impact and presence by providing upskilling workshops, mentoring, leadership & professional development opportunities, visibility, networking, and community-building platforms and programs.

At UNITED LATINAS we know that finding community and building professional alliances can be a powerful source of growth and inspiration. That's why we strive to create a space where Latinas from around the globe can come together and find commonality, support, and encouragement.

At UNITED LATINAS, we believe that Latinas deserve to be seen and heard. We work to amplify the voices of our community, increase their visibility, and expand their leadership presence and impact. Whether you're a seasoned leader or just starting out, we offer a variety of development programs, visibility platforms and resources to help you upskill and grow.

OUR PILLARS

Leadership & Business Upskill

We offer leadership and business development training programs to help Latinas reach their full potential. From corporate confidence building to practical business planning, our programs are designed to help Latina entrepreneurs and side hustlers grow and succeed.

Visibility & Recognition

We prioritize the visibility and recognition of Latinas. We work to amplify the voices of our community and increase their leadership presence and impact by providing safe spaces, like the Latina Speakers Club, for public speaking and sharing powerful messages.

Community & Network

Find a sense of belonging and build professional alliances with other Latinas from around the globe. We strive to create a supportive and inclusive environment where you can feel valued and encouraged to leave a lasting legacy.

Ready to take the next step in your leadership journey? Join us and discover the power of connecting with other like-minded Latinas!

www.unitedlatinas.com

hello@unitedlatinas.com

UNITED LATINAS Mighty Hub
Your Gateway to a Powerful UL Online Experience
https://unitedlatinas.mn.com

ABOUT THE PUBLISHING AUTHORS

ILHIANA ROJAS SALDANA

ILHIANA ROJAS SALDANA is a Human Potential & Culture Expert, an Award-Winning Advancing Women & Hispanics Advocate, an Executive and Leadership Coach, a DEIB Consultant, a seasoned multicultural Business Strategist, a Bestselling Publishing Author, and an International Motivational Speaker.

Ilhiana has over 20 years of global executive experience in top Fortune 500 companies in Mexico and US headquarters, leading and coaching professionals, teams, and businesses into success. As the founder of her first company BeLIVE Coaching and Consulting, Ilhiana is a certified expert in leadership and DEIB best practices that help build resilient, collaborative, and high-performing leaders and cultures. Ilhiana has mentored and coached leaders of all levels and has delivered impactful coaching programs to over 3500 professionals across multiple industries and sectors worldwide.

Her strong commitment to advocating for equity led her to co-launch a second company UNITED LATINAS Corp, leading as Co-President. UNITED LATINAS is a women's empowerment and leadership development organization providing upskilling workshops, mentoring opportunities, leadership and professional development programs, visibility, networking, and community-building platforms and programs. She has also been the driving force in the launch of four women's leadership development programs in Europe, LAM, and the US to reduce the gender gap, and has been the publishing author of two Best-selling Anthology books, sharing the stories of 30 Latina leaders.

Before starting her two companies, Ilhiana was a highly respected global business leader and seasoned strategist with extensive multicultural experience driving transformational change through deep consumer understanding, developing breakthrough business strategies, and building high-performing and engaging cultures. She has played key leadership roles in companies including P&G, Hanesbrands, and Hasbro, acquiring a strong understanding of consumers of all ages, genders, ethnic and cultural backgrounds. During this time, Ilhiana drove double-digit growth across numerous businesses and returned a business to profitability after years of net losses, and earned several recognitions and awards for her strategy, innovation, and positive team culture.

In addition to coaching, Ilhiana is actively involved in different diversity, equity & inclusion initiatives with a focus on empowering women and the Hispanic population in the corporate and non-profit sectors. She currently serves as Chief Development Officer for ALPFA (Association of Latino Professionals for America) Boston Chapter, and a Founding Board Member for Thousand Faces and GetWise. She also serves as an advisor for the Rhode Island Hispanic Chamber of Commerce, the Center for Women & Enterprise (CWE), Social Enterprise Greenhouse (SEG) and several other private organizations and institutions. Furthermore, she is an Executive MBA Career Advisor for the Hult International Business School.

Ilhiana's most notable awards and recognitions include the 2023 P&G Alumni D&I Award, the 2023 Top Coaches Award by WomELLE, the 2022 Women in Business Stevie Gold Award, the NY Journal 2021 Top 10 Inspiring Women to Watch, ALPFA (Association of Latino Professionals for America) 2021 Latina to Watch, and 2020 Amplify LatinX' Amplifier Honoree.

Ilhiana graduated with honors as a Chemical Engineer in Mexico City, and lives in Rhode Island with her husband and two kids.

Learn more and connect with Ilhiana at:

www.belivecoach.com
ww.ilhianarojas.com
https://www.linkedin.com/in/ilhiana-rojas7
ilhiana@unitedlatinas.com

SANDRA NOEMI TORRES

Sandra Noemi Torres is a dynamic Public Speaker and seasoned Marketing and Business Strategist with over 20 years of consulting and scaling small and medium sized business owners and entrepreneurs.

Sandra has managed multi seven figure ad marketing budgets and is an expert in strategies that connect, convert and build customer loyalty. With a focus on high-impact and results-driven solutions, she has earned a reputation as a trusted advisor and key decision maker in mission-critical brand messaging campaigns.

Sandra is the Founder and CEO for UNITED LATINAS, a thriving women's personal development organization that empowers Latina women, She spearheaded the creation of Latina Speakers Club, a leading Latina Speakers Directory where Hispanic women are showcased and highlighted and promoted as the thought leaders they are.

Sandra is also the Founder and CEO of Sandra Noemi & Co, dba/ Plan Your Company, a full service digital marketing agency with coaching and consulting services, Sandra brings her years of expertise in marketing, sales, business development strategies to every project and every conversation she takes on.

Sandra is a two-time published author with her book The Life Agreement and a collaborative project & #1 Amazon Best Seller through United Latinas, Extraordinary Latinas Vol II - Breaking The Narrative & Redefining Our Power. And the creator of the MindCreatesMatter Series of Books that will be released in 2024, that helps Individuals, Entrepreneurs and Marketing professionals help reach their goals

Learn more and connect with Sandra at:

https://www.linkedin.com/in/sandratorres/
https://planyourcompany.com/

www.ingramcontent.com/pod-product-compliance
Lightning Source LLC
Chambersburg PA
CBHW060017100426
42740CB00010B/1507